THE GUIDE TO

COLORADO WINERIES

SECOND EDITION

ALTA AND BRAD SMITH

FULCRUM PUBLISHING
GOLDEN, COLORADO

The information in *The Guide to Colorado Wineries* is accurate as of January 2002. However, information regarding prices, hours of operations, street and e-mail addresses, phone numbers, websites and other items change rapidly. If something in this book is incorrect, please write to the authors in care of Fulcrum Publishing, 16100 Table Mountain Parkway, Suite 300, Golden, CO 80403; fulcrum@fulcrum-books.com.

The Guide to Colorado Wineries provides many tips about travel and alcohol consumption, but good decision making and sound judgment are the responsibility of the individual. Neither the publisher nor the authors assume any liability for injury that may arise from the use of this book.

Library of Congress Cataloging-in-Publication Data

Smith, Alta.
The guide to Colorado wineries / Alta Smith and Brad Smith.—2nd ed.
p. cm.
Includes bibliographical references and index.
ISBN 1-55591-314-8 (Paperback)
1. Wine and wine making—Colorado—Guidebooks. 2. Wineries—Colorado—Guidebooks. 3. Colorado—Guidebooks. I. Smith, Brad. II. Title.
TP557 .S55 2002
641.2'2'09788—dc21

2001006765

Printed in Canada
0 9 8 7 6 5 4 3 2 1

Editorial: Daniel Forrest-Bank, Marlene Blessing
Cover and interior design: Jennifer LaRock Shontz
Cover painting of wine bottle label: Mindy Dwyer
Cover photograph: Nancy Duncan-Cashman
Maps: Courtesy of the Colorado Wine Industry Development Board. Original map design by Amy Nuernberg; updated by Hill and Company Integrated Marketing

Fulcrum Publishing
16100 Table Mountain Parkway, Suite 300
Golden, Colorado 80403
(800) 992-2908 • (303) 277-1623
www.fulcrum-books.com

CONTENTS

Mountain Wineries

Front Range Wineries

Recipes from the Wineries

ACKNOWLEDGMENTS

THE AUTHORS OWE A GREAT DEAL to the many people who have helped and encouraged us with this book. Foremost are the owners and winemakers at all of Colorado's wineries. They have been most generous with their time, even during very busy periods. Without their kind assistance this book would not have been possible. We also want to thank Doug Caskey, executive director of the Colorado Wine Industry Development Board, who has met with us several times and shared his insights. The board also was kind enough to share its maps of the wineries. Also, we appreciate the encouragement and assistance of Marlene Blessing, Daniel Forrest-Bank and everyone else at Fulcrum Publishing. Many of our friends also helped us taste the recipes as well as the wine.

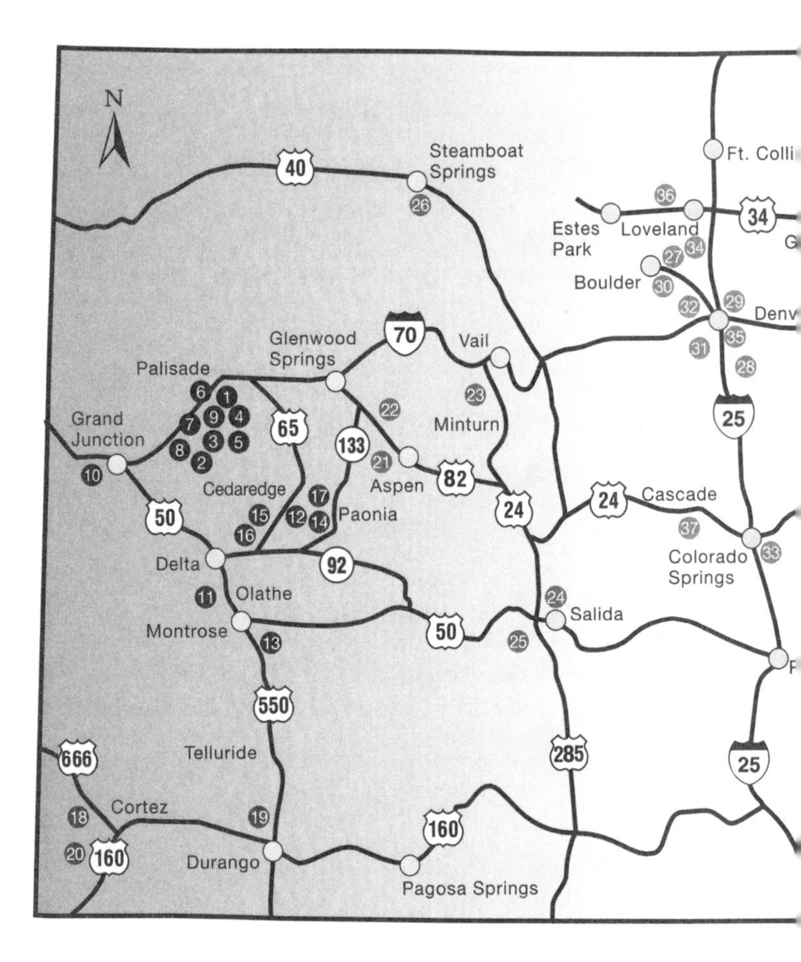
N
Steamboat
Springs
Ft. Colli
Estes
Park
Loveland
G
Boulder
Denv
Glenwood
Springs
Vail
Palisade
Minturn
Grand
Junction
Aspen
Cedaredge
Paonia
Cascade
Colorado
Springs
Delta
Olathe
Montrose
Salida
Telluride
Cortez
Durango
Pagosa Springs

Grand Valley

1. Canyon Wind Cellars
2. Carlson Vineyards
3. Colorado Cellars
4. Corley Vineyards
5. DeBeque Canyon Winery
6. Grande River Vineyards
7. Plum Creek Cellars
8. Rocky Mountain Meadery
9. St. Kathryn Cellars*
10. Two Rivers Winery

Delta & Montrose Counties

11. Cottonwood Cellars
12. Red Mountain Ranches*
13. Rocky Hill Winery
14. S. Rhodes Vineyards
15. Stoney Mesa Winery
16. Surface Creek Winery
17. Terror Creek Winery

Four Corners

18. Guy Drew Vineyards
19. Honeyville*
20. Sutcliffe Vineyards

Rocky Mountains

21. Aspen Valley Winery
22. Baharav Vineyards
23. Minturn Cellars
24. Mountain Spirit Gallery*
25. Mountain Spirit Winery, Ltd.
26. Steamboat Springs Cellars

Front Range

27. Augustina's Winery
28. Avanti Winery*
29. J. A. Balistreri Vineyards
30. Bookcliff Vineyards
31. Creekside Cellars
32. Old Town Winery
33. Pikes Peak Vineyards
34. Redstone Meadery
35. Tewksbury & Co.*
36. Trail Ridge Winery
37. Wines of Colorado*

* Tasting room only

Note: Garfield Estates Vineyards is not on this map.

INTRODUCTION

WHEN WE WROTE THE FIRST EDITION of our book in 1997, the Colorado wine industry was in the midst of an explosion, but no one knew how big the boom was going to be. In 1990, there were just four wineries, and when our book came out there were sixteen. As we write this second edition that number has more than doubled to thirty-eight, and we know of several more that may open in the coming years. The American Vintners Association says Colorado's wine industry had the fastest growth of any state with more than one winery during the 1990s.

Still, putting things in perspective, Colorado's wine industry is tiny, compared to giants such as California, where more than half the country's 2,100 wineries are located. There are wineries in every state except Alaska, and Colorado is well down the list of major producers. Colorado ranks thirty-seventh in wine grape acreage with just over 500 acres, according to Horst Gaspari, the viticulturist at the Orchard Mesa Research Center, operated by Colorado State University near Grand Junction. Even Idaho has more than three times the acreage of Colorado.

Colorado also doesn't have a single giant winery such as California's Mondavi. The majority of the state's wineries are essentially boutique operations and small farms. The largest producers, among the wineries that provide their output, are Plum Creek Cellars with an annual output of 18,000–30,000 gallons and Colorado Cellars with 25,000 gallons annually. The smallest are Avanti Winery (more a tasting room than a winery, at least for now) with 90 gallons and Reeder Mesa Vineyards with 480 gallons.

From our point of view, the small size is actually one of the main attractions of Colorado's wine industry. Because these are small operations, they also are very personal. Each one has a distinct character as a business, and most of their wines reflect the owner's personality. In every case, the owner is either the winemaker or is very involved in the winemaking and, often, in growing the grapes as well.

GRAND VALLEY—
THE HEART OF WINE COUNTRY

Colorado's wine grape-growing industry is centered on the Western Slope, with about 90 percent of the state's grapes coming from Mesa and Delta Counties and the vast majority coming from Mesa. That may change slightly as farmers experiment in other areas of the state. The most popular wine grape varieties (known by the Latin name *Vitis vinifera*) historically have done the best in those areas because of the relatively mild winters and long growing seasons. The Palisade region, east of Grand Junction, is a hot spot for grape vineyards as well as peach orchards. Winter hardiness is the key to grape survival in the state and is the reason you don't find many wine grapes along the Front Range, although some intrepid growers are producing.

The high altitude gives Colorado the distinction of having the country's (and perhaps the world's) highest winery, Terror Creek Winery near Paonia at 6,400 feet. The altitude also impacts the grapes grown in the state. At this elevation the sunlight is intense and there are large daily temperature fluctuations you don't find at lower altitudes. Because of this, Colorado's grapes are naturally rich in color and high in acid content, both of which are desirable in making wine.

Although western Colorado's growing season isn't as long as some other states, which means some late-maturing grape varieties can't be grown here, there is one positive result. Frost actually is more of a danger in California than it is in Colorado because vines in Colorado don't begin flowering until May when the frost danger is lower, according to *The Colorado Grape Growers Guide*, put out by the Cooperative Extension Resource Center at Colorado State University–Fort Collins. Still, Colorado has a shorter growing season than regions at a lower elevation.

So, which grapes are best for Colorado? Since the industry is still young, the question probably won't be decided for some time. But there are varieties that do better here than others. In an effort to find an answer to the question, the CSU Orchard Mesa Research Center, the main viticulture research facility in the state, grows thirty-five different grape varieties, the vast majority of which are traditional *Vitis vinifera*.

In recent years, Merlot has been the predominant grape and wine in Colorado, followed by Chardonnay. In most years, the state's altitude provides a Merlot that is deep-colored, fruity and full-bodied. Chardonnay had been the leader, but many of the Chardonnay vines were hit both by an early freeze and late frost in the late 1990s.

Cabernet Sauvignon, Cabernet Franc and Riesling also are popular grapes that seem to do well in the state. In recent years, several wineries have added a Lemberger to their repertoire, although its strange name (sometimes confused with a type of cheese) often is not prominent on the label. Other leading grape varieties include Gewürztraminer, Sauvignon Blanc, Pinot Noir and Shiraz/Syrah. Viognier has become popular among some wineries. Another trend is Port-style wines.

One grape that is popular in California, but not often found in Colorado, is Zinfandel, which needs a longer growing season than the state offers. Only a few wineries offer Zinfandel.

Some vineyards are also experimenting with hybrid grapes, many developed for cold climates. Among these are Cayuga, Seyval Blanc and Chardonel. Dr. Richard Smart, an Australian viticulturist brought to the state in 2000 by the Colorado Wine Industry Development Board, suggested growers might consider growing the Tempranillo grape, the principal grape in Spain's famous "Rioja" wines. At least one grower, Plum Creek Cellars, has produced wines from Sangiovese grapes, the main grape in Italy's Chianti.

The owners of two of the state's oldest wineries—Doug Phillips at Plum Creek Cellars and Stephen Smith of Grande River Vineyards—believe that Merlot will ultimately be Colorado's signature grape and wine. Smith has the largest vineyard in the state, 60 acres, and believes so strongly in Merlot that one-third of his acreage is devoted to the grape. "In the long run people will look at Palisade as a place for red grapes," Phillips says. "We're in our infancy now, but in fifteen to twenty years Merlot will be the red grape."

Tim Merrick, the owner-winemaker at Trail Ridge Winery, salutes the Colorado Wine Industry Development Board and Executive Director Doug Caskey for trying to improve the quality of the state's wines. Instead of attacking the bad wineries, Merrick says, the board has emphasized raising the quality, spending $40,000 in recent years to do so. This included bringing in a paid wine consultant, Richard Bruno, owner of Vinum Cellars Winery in California. Bruno spent up to two days with each winery at a cost of $80 per day, giving winery-specific advice on how realistically to improve their quality.

Asked about how this is affecting Colorado's wine industry, Tim says, "It's still uneven, but more good than bad. We've got more resources now. More established wineries are consistently turning out quality wines in greater volume."

It appears that this attention to quality is especially evident among some of the newest wineries. Many of these new wineries, especially in the Grand Valley, are bent on bringing their own distinctive styles to the wines. An example is Garfield Estates Vineyards, whose owners are calling in outside expertise and using innovative techniques.

OLDEST NOT YET OLD

The oldest existing winery in Colorado is Colorado Cellars, founded under the name Colorado Mountain Vineyards in 1978. But the state's wine history goes back more than a century. Then, as now, the grapes were primarily grown in the Grand Valley area along the Colorado River. The 1899 U.S. Census says the state produced 1,744 gallons of wine that year and among the early growers was Governor George Crawford.

Prohibition ended Colorado's small wine industry in 1916, when the state legislature enacted a prohibition statute four years before the nation, and the vines were replaced with fruit trees. Colorado's wine industry lay dormant until 1968, when Gerald Ivancie established a winery under his name and planted wine grapes in the Grand Valley.

CSU's Orchard Mesa Research Center opened in 1974, and in 1977 the Colorado Legislature passed a law allowing small farm wineries. In 1990, the Colorado Wine Industry Development Board, funded by a tax on the wineries, was created to promote the state's industry. Also in 1990, the Grand Valley was granted the federal designation as an American Viticulture Area, giving it increased credibility. The state's second AVA, called the West Elks in eastern Delta County, was granted in 2001.

The vast majority of grapes are grown on the Western Slope, but wineries have mushroomed across the state. Pikes Peak Vineyards, founded in Colorado in 1983, was the only Front Range winery for years, but now is one of ten, many of which have sprouted in the Denver–Boulder area. There soon will be six in the mountains, including three in the Aspen area. And they're popping up in remote areas such as the McElmo Canyon area in far southwestern Colorado. The Grand Valley between Palisade and Grand Junction has the largest concentration with twelve wineries.

Stephen Smith believes Colorado's wine industry has reached a critical mass necessary to create momentum for continued growth both in production and wineries. There is limited acreage on which to grow wine grapes in the state, so it likely will never reach the size of Washington state. Some think it could become another Oregon, which is dominated by small wineries and is known for its Pinot Noir wines. CSU's Gaspari says a maximum of 2,000–3,000 acres could realistically be planted in grapes, which is four to six times the current acreage.

WINE CONSUMPTION GROWTH

More people are drinking Colorado wines than ever before. A survey by the Wine Industry Development Board showed an 8 percent increase in market share in 2000, although general consumption still amounts to fewer than one bottle out of every 100 bottles sold. The 505,000 bottles of Colorado wine sold in 2000 had a retail value of 5 million dollars.

The wine board has brought viticulturalists, such as Richard Smart, and oenologists, such as Richard Bruno of California, to help raise the quality of the state's wines. Despite these programs, some winery owners think it is not enough. Fred Strothman, owner of Rocky Mountain Meadery and St. Kathryn Cellars, believes the state needs to establish its own in-state oenology research facility. A former judge, Strothman created a furor in the wine industry in 2001 by filing a lawsuit against dozens of liquor sellers, distributors and trade groups alleging they threatened to boycott him if he sold wine at Vail's City Market grocery store. Although wine cannot be sold in the state's grocery stores, Strothman set up a separate facility inside the store from which shoppers could buy wine as they left. Strothman included four other wineries as defendants in his suit. The case was still in court when this book was written.

Another suit in the mid-1990s also created friction in the industry. Rick Turley, owner of Colorado Cellars, said his constitutional rights were violated because he was forced to pay an excise tax to the wine board. The suit ended with the retention of the 1-cent-per-liter tax, but representation on the wine board was broadened to include more members and regions, including a four-year term for Turley.

TASTING WINE

Although we will not recommend wines, we will recommend how to taste them, based on generally accepted guidelines. You may notice in the descriptions of the wineries that we don't list which ones may have won awards, believing not all awards are equal and some choose not to enter competitions. But the wineries will happily share those with you.

You don't have to follow our wine-tasting tips, but if you are interested in learning more about the differences among wines they may help. The steps can roughly be described as "look," "swirl," "smell" and "taste." Note that the first three steps occur before anything is put in the mouth. The final and fourth step involves the tongue's ability to taste four things: salt, sweet, bitter and sour, though you should not taste salt in a wine.

Pour a small amount of wine in a clear glass and hold it against the light, tipping the glass to look through the rim so you can see the variation in colors. Few white wines are truly white; more often they have yellow or green hues. Red wines may have brown or purple highlights. Look for clarity; a lack thereof probably means suspended particles, or sediment left if a wine is not filtered.

Now swirl the wine in the glass. This does two things. One, it releases more aroma from within the wine, and two, it creates a thin transparent film on the inside of the glass, usually referred to as "legs," because the liquid falls unevenly down the glass. Some people believe "legs" are important as an illustration of quality, but they are merely a function of the viscosity, or stickiness caused by mixing alcohol and glycerin.

Smell is perhaps the most difficult part of tasting because that is where the brain registers the complexities of the wine. Scientists estimate that the human nose can register as many as 10,000 different smells. There are textbooks and courses devoted to the subject of smelling wine. This is where you will hear a lot of the "wine talk" that insiders use. Don't be intimidated. Like anything else, it is a learning process. Don't undertake it to impress anyone; rather, try to distinguish the smells so your nose can become better educated and you can become a more sophisticated wine drinker.

There are too many aromas in wine to name here. Suffice it to say that just about every fruit, especially berry fruit, is associated with one kind of wine or another. Other common aromas are herbs, vegetables, earth, flowers, honey, vanilla and grass. These aromas can help you identify the wine and its character. After sniffing, take a small sip of wine. Be aware that the tongue tastes different sensations in different places. The first sensation will be the level of sweetness. Purse your lips and pull in a small amount of air across your tongue. This helps to release the vapors in the wine. Roll the wine around in your mouth. You'll get a sensation of how dense ("chewy") the wine is. On the sides of the mouth you may taste the astringency of the wine's tannins—what some winemakers have described as a "furry" taste. At the back of the mouth you'll taste the alcohol level. Any sourness you taste is related to the amount of acid in the wine, which gives it a tingle. The best wines generally balance all these tastes so no single characteristic stands out.

When you swallow, notice the finish or how your mouth feels after swallowing. If you exhale slightly some of the aroma will enter the lower part of the nasal passage. Some experienced tasters may take a minute for this part. What you are looking for throughout this process is a balance of all these various qualities. In many wines, one quality stands out, such as overwhelming fruitiness. Really good wines let you discover the subtle differences of each component.

AUTHORS' THOUGHTS

The Guide to Colorado Wineries is a guidebook on just that—discovering the state's wineries, their owners, the winemakers and their wines. With that in mind, we believe that the enjoyment of wine is a subjective experience and that you, the reader, are the best judge of the wines you like.

We have another fundamental belief: wine and food go together, with one enhancing the enjoyment of the other. Therefore, we have included recipes, grouped together in the back of the book, nearly all of which were contributed by the wineries themselves. Alta has tested all these recipes in the kitchen and has added her notes to most of them. We encourage you to try the recipes with the wines. You may discover some new taste treats. See for yourself the amazing effect that food has on the taste of wine.

Finally, we have found we enjoy wine more when we have been to the winery that made it. There's something about having visited the winery, perhaps meeting and talking with the winemaker and/or owner, that adds something to the taste of the wine once you are back in your own home. In addition, finding these wineries can be an adventure in itself, taking you to parts of Colorado you might never have visited otherwise. Both of us have lived in Colorado most of our lives and thought we had seen it all. Since undertaking the research for this book, we have discovered, through these wineries, that there are always new vistas waiting to be discovered.

In the back of the book is a short glossary of terms for those who want to know more about the words used to describe wine and the process of wine-making. But you don't need to know these words to know what you like. If you want to explore the wine world further, there are numerous wine books explaining the intricacies of wine-making and wine-tasting, as well as classes on these subject areas. We've listed some of our favorites.

Besides visiting the winery, one of the best ways to explore Colorado wines is through festivals and wine-tastings. We've included a list of some of the more popular ones in the back of the book. When you visit the winery or go to a tasting, take our book along because there is a list of each winery's product and space to keep your own notes and ratings. We haven't listed vintages or descriptions because these change and are available at each winery. Ask the wineries for food serving suggestions.

At the end of each section we have included a few of the places we have stayed, some that are not listed in other guidebooks, as well as a few suggestions of places you might want to eat that would add to your enjoyment. For a broader treatment of travel around the state, we encourage you to read *The Colorado Guide, Fifth Edition* by Bruce Caughey and Dean Winstanley (Fulcrum Publishing, 2001).

We think visiting the winery itself is the best discovery of all and invite you to take the adventure yourself. Happy wine hunting and good tasting!

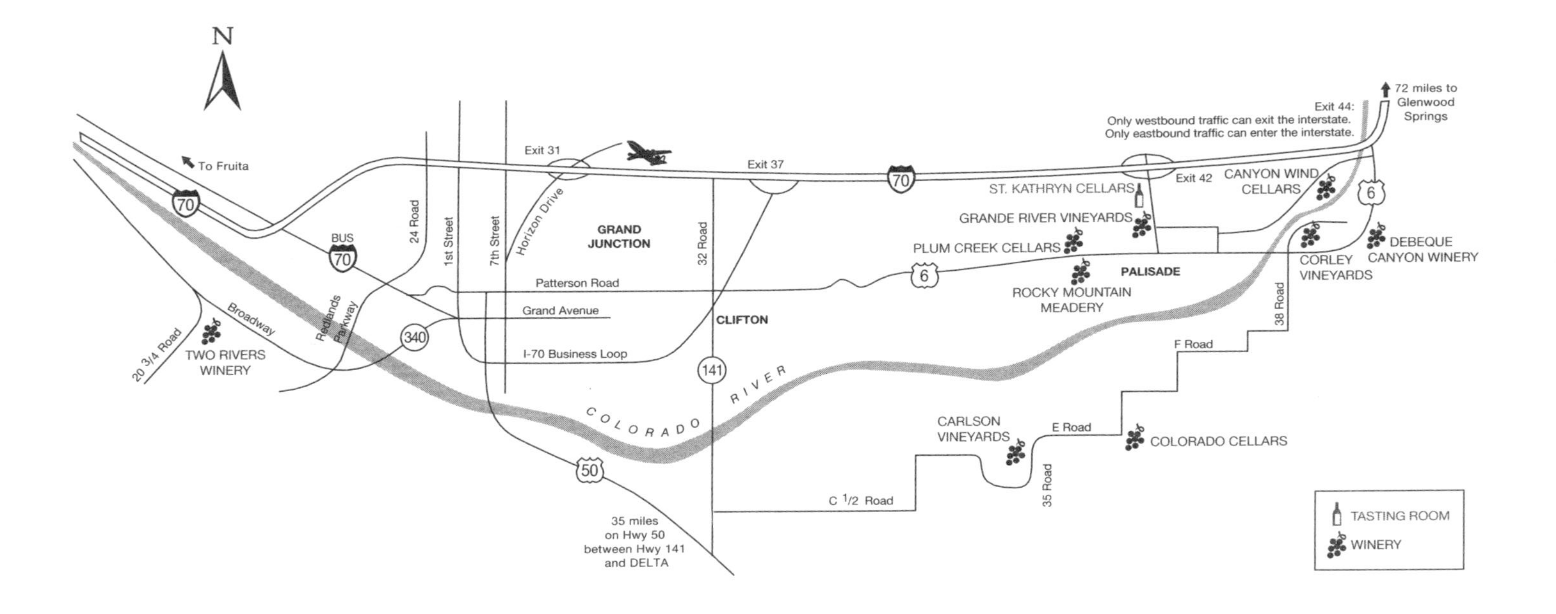
N
To Fruita
72 miles to Glenwood Springs
Exit 44:
Only westbound traffic can exit the interstate.
Only eastbound traffic can enter the interstate.
Exit 31
Exit 37
Exit 42
70
BUS 70
6
50
141
340
24 Road
1st Street
7th Street
Horizon Drive
GRAND JUNCTION
32 Road
Patterson Road
Grand Avenue
I-70 Business Loop
CLIFTON
PALISADE
Broadway
Redlands Parkway
20 3/4 Road
TWO RIVERS WINERY
COLORADO RIVER
ST. KATHRYN CELLARS
GRANDE RIVER VINEYARDS
PLUM CREEK CELLARS
ROCKY MOUNTAIN MEADERY
CANYON WIND CELLARS
CORLEY VINEYARDS
DEBEQUE CANYON WINERY
38 Road
F Road
E Road
35 Road
C 1/2 Road
CARLSON VINEYARDS
COLORADO CELLARS
35 miles on Hwy 50 between Hwy 141 and DELTA
TASTING ROOM
WINERY

GRAND VALLEY WINERIES

Canyon Wind Cellars

OWNERS' NAMES: Norman and Ellen Christianson
WINEMAKER: Robert Pepi
YEAR LICENSED: 1996
ADDRESS: 3907 North River Road, Palisade, Colorado 81526
TELEPHONE: 970-464-0888
WEBSITE: N/A
TASTING ROOM HOURS: 10 A.M.–5 P.M., Monday–Saturday
WINE AVAILABILITY OUTSIDE WINERY: Distributed locally throughout Colorado, seven other states and Great Britain. Will ship to legal states.

PRICE RANGE OF WINES SOLD AT WINERY: $11.95–$19.95 for wine; $16.00–$30.00 for Port

WINE CLUB: Yes

ANNUAL PRODUCTION: 10,000 gallons

DIRECTIONS TO THE WINERY: Approaching Palisade on I-70 from the west take Exit 44. Stay right across the bridge for 0.6 mile and winery is on the south side of the road. The Palisade Greenhouse borders the winery property on the west. From Palisade, take 3rd Street east, and the winery is three-fourths of a mile from the city limits.

FACILITIES AND AMENITIES: Tasting room. Picnic tables under a tree. Tours on Friday and Saturday at 11 A.M., 1 P.M. and 3 P.M.

When we wrote our first edition in 1997, Canyon Wind Cellars was the new kid on the block with one wine, a Chardonnay. There was a lot of anticipation about its wines at the time. Norm and Ellen Christianson came into the wine industry with a desire to make quality wines for a sophisticated audience and to "raise the bar" among Colorado's wineries. To many, it has lived up to those expectations.

Norm, a former geologist involved like several other Colorado wine figures in the oil and gas business, researched his 50-acre site before buying at the mouth of DeBeque Canyon, just east of Palisade. About half the land is planted in grapes. "It's in a weather pocket, partly because of the winds [from the canyon] so the cold doesn't come up this far," he says. Those favorable winds gave the winery its name.

The Christiansons also hired Robert Pepi as their winemaker and consultant. Pepi is well known in the California wine industry, having owned his own winery for years before becoming a consultant. The Christiansons are concentrating on just three wines: Chardonnay, Merlot and Cabernet Sauvignon. In addition, they produce a Port-style made from Cabernet Sauvignon, which was introduced in 2000.

As the twenty-first century unfolded, Canyon Wind tripled the size of the winery by adding a new cold storage facility with underground barrel storage and a fully automated, state-of-the-art Italian bottling system. The bottling line cleans the bottles, fills them, inserts the cork, caps them and attaches the labels. "Sterile bottling eliminates many of the things that can go wrong [with winemaking]," Christianson says.

Norm, whose size reminds one of John Wayne, believes that by making quality wine he will help the whole industry. He says he doesn't want to make "tourist wines." In 1997, his tasting room was open by appointment only, but in 2000 the winery added regular staffing and hours for direct sales. He also is aiming for wider distribution. "We want a diversified base and we're intent on making fine wine. People (referring especially to Californians) are always looking for new wines. We want to be a regional wine, but also be in metro areas where there are sophisticated palates." In 2001, his wines could be found in seven states plus Great Britain. The latter, Norm says, because he has friends there who wanted to be able to buy his wines.

In the future, the Christiansons hope to double their production from the current 4,000 cases, but will not get any bigger than that. "We don't want to lose that individual contact with the wine," he says. "You can keep quality up that way."

Canyon Wind is off by itself east of Palisade, but you'll have no trouble finding it along North River Road just east of the Palisade Greenhouse facility. Turn right (south) at the Canyon Wind sign on the road, drive down the dirt road between the rows of grapevines. Park and walk through the rock-walled front yard on a cobblestone-like path and into the small, but well-appointed tasting room. If you've brought a picnic or snack, sit under the expansive tree in front and enjoy the breeze!

WINE LIST

Cabernet Sauvignon
Chardonnay
Merlot
Port

Carlson Vineyards

OWNERS' NAMES: Mary and Parker Carlson
WINEMAKER: Parker Carlson
YEAR LICENSED: 1988
ADDRESS: 461 35 Road, Palisade, Colorado 81526
TELEPHONE: 970-464-5554 or 888-464-5554
WEBSITE: www.carlsonvineyards.com
TASTING ROOM HOURS: 10 A.M.–6 P.M. daily
WINE AVAILABILITY OUTSIDE WINERY: In liquor stores throughout Colorado and some restaurants; will ship to states where allowed by law.
PRICE RANGE OF WINES SOLD AT WINERY: $7.99–$12.99
WINE CLUB: Yes (see website)
ANNUAL PRODUCTION: 15,000 gallons

DIRECTIONS TO THE WINERY: Take I-70 to Exit 42 at Palisade. From exit, drive south into Palisade and turn left on Front Street (Highway 6). As soon as you cross the river, turn right on 38 Road. Follow that road through eight 90-degree turns or about 5.5 miles while road names change. The winery is on the right (west) side of road with a sign over the mailbox in the shape of a large wine bottle.

FACILITIES AND AMENITIES: Tasting room and a backyard picnic area with grass and shade.

One of the oldest wineries in the state, Carlson Vineyards planted their first grapes in 1981 and opened their winery in 1988. They were first known for their fruit wines, including a cherry wine, the sales of which went up by 50 percent in 2000. That increase could have happened because on the weekends Mary Carlson serves it in glasses dipped in chocolate made by Enstrom Candies in Grand Junction.

Together with her husband, winemaker Parker Carlson, it's obvious to see they have a warm sense of humor and much fun with their wine. You'll find charming labels with imaginative names reflecting their proximity to Dinosaur National Monument such as "Pearadactyl."

While the labels may be amusing, the winemaking is serious. These wines are fruity, soft and drinkable, often Beaujolais style. Their Tyrannosaurus Red, which is all Lemberger (note: not the cheese), has sold so well that Parker is going to plant more. "It's been our largest selling red; it's the most distinct," Parker says.

New in 2000 was their premium wine label, Cougar Run. The label is a graphic by Amy Nuernberg, based on a petroglyph the Carlsons saw in the Petrified Forest in Arizona.

"We like cats," Mary says, "We fell in love with it. It looks modern as well."

The first release was at the 2000 Winefest, the Cougar Run Merlot/Shiraz, and they sold fifty cases that day. Parker told us, "I've always liked Shiraz; it's a great blending grape. I want to be associated with the Aussie style, which is fruity and down-to-earth, like us, not like the French Syrah. So we'll keep the Shiraz name."

These new premium wines should answer the wine snobs (some scoffed at their other wines because they were fruit wines, because they had cute labels, or for the easy drinkability of their first line).

When asked about their future and that of the Colorado wine industry, Mary says she thinks the industry is growing like "gangbusters" but will never be like California's Napa Valley because it doesn't have enough growing room.

"When we started getting more wineries, we didn't worry about losing our piece of the pie," she says. "It didn't hurt us, and they have to find their niche."

The future for the Carlsons is not to get much bigger. They may sell the winery to a grower family and retire in five years or so. Parker, an avid amateur archaeologist, would like to learn to cook and fish, and Mary would probably like a little rest from tractor-riding, vine-tending and selling.

For you, however, it's a pleasant country drive to Carlson Vineyards, zigzagging through the orchards and small farms. Before entering, you might see Mary filling her hummingbird feeders or Parker walking down from his vineyards. You'll easily recognize him with his suspenders, gray beard and jolly expression. He's been referred to as the poster child for the Colorado wine industry. Even though this notoriety is sometimes embarrassing to him, he enjoys it.

When you enter the tasting room, you'll be greeted warmly by staff or the owners. "We like to hang out in our tasting room," Mary says. "We like people. People say, 'You're the owner?' We like to treat them like visiting family, not customers. We want them to come back." Maybe that's the reason they sell more than half of their wine out of the tasting room. Put your elbows on their tasting room's cool granite bar top and taste some wine. You're welcome here.

WINE LIST

Chardonnay (Cougar Run)
Gewürztraminer
Merlot (Cougar Run label)
Merlot/Shiraz (Cougar Run label)
Prairie Dog Blush
Riesling
Shiraz/Cabernet
Sunny Dale White
Tyrannosaurus Red

Fruit Wines

Cherry
Pearadactyl
Plum

Colorado Cellars

OWNERS' NAMES: Richard and Padte Turley
WINEMAKER: Padte Turley
YEAR LICENSED: 1978
ADDRESS: 3553 E Road, Palisade, Colorado 81526
TELEPHONE: 970-464-7921
WEBSITE: N/A
TASTING ROOM HOURS: Monday–Friday 9 A.M.–4 P.M.; Saturday 11:30 A.M.–4 P.M. year-round
WINE AVAILABILITY OUTSIDE WINERY: Distributed widely in Colorado. Will ship to legal states.
PRICE RANGE OF WINES SOLD AT WINERY: $7.50–$20.00
WINE CLUB: No
ANNUAL PRODUCTION: 25,000 gallons
DIRECTIONS TO THE WINERY: From I-70, take Exit 37 (Highway 141) south to C½ Road, east 5.6 miles, following curves.
FACILITIES AND AMENITIES: Tasting room and 0.5 acre of grass with two gazebos. About three dozen wine-based food items available in the tasting room.

Getting to Colorado's oldest existing winery can be a lesson in math and the ABCs and might be difficult for a first-timer to remember. But it's really quite straightforward if you put your mind to it. That's because whoever laid out the roads in Mesa County had a very logical thought process, assigning letters for east–west roads and numbers for north–south roads (the latter start with "1" on the Colorado–Utah border and goes east from there). When new roads were added between the letters and numbers, though, you come up with decimal roads, like G.25 Road. This mathematical precision is evident driving from Palisade to Colorado Cellars. There is no straight path anywhere on East Orchard Mesa—nearly every curve is 90 degrees.

Colorado Cellars owners Rick and Padte Turley recommend another route to their winery (see their directions above), which may be faster. Still, we prefer the scenic route for sightseeing.

Pick up the scenic route from Palisade's main east–west Front Street (Highway 6). Head east across the Colorado River bridge and almost immediately take 38 Road going south. Follow the road as it twists and turns—and changes names according to mathematical formulas—until you come to a 90-degree curve where southbound 35½ Road becomes westbound E Road. Instead of turning west on E Road you turn left onto a dirt road and then quickly to the right again. You'll see the adobe-colored winery at the foot of the mesa above.

You won't be able to drive very fast through East Orchard Mesa, giving you time to look at the orchards for which the mesa is named, the new vineyards and a number of fruit stands where you can buy fruit in-season.

The Turleys have owned Colorado Cellars since 1989, but the winery has been in existence since 1978 when it was founded as Colorado Mountain Vineyards by about thirty investors. Although boasting one of the state's largest wine productions, about 25,000 gallons, it is very much a family operation that involves not only Rick and Padte but also their two sons, Corey and Kyle.

The 6,800-square foot winery is on two levels, with the wine store on the second. After you walk up to the front door, stop for one of the best views in the area—to the north are Mount Garfield and the Bookcliffs, to the east is Grand Mesa. Three of the Turley's 20 acres of vineyards are here—the other 17 acres are several miles west near U.S. 50.

Colorado Cellars has one of the widest selections of wines in the state, as well as an intriguing array of food and wine products. Their store has herb wines for cooking, such as Chardonnay

Parsley/Sage, plus grilling sauces, pasta, dessert toppings and several kinds of grape seed oil. Padte has recipe suggestions on the back labels of many bottles.

For most of its existence, Colorado Cellars used some non-Colorado grapes in its wines but since 1997 has exclusively used grapes grown in the state. Most of its wines carry the distinctive Colorado Cellars label, an artist's rendition of Mount Crested Butte based on a photo taken by Rick, but it has two other labels as well. Its number one–selling wine, an off-dry RoadKill Red, is under the Rocky Mountain Vineyards label. It has a champagne-style sparkling wine under a Colorado Mountain Vineyards label.

Padte is the winemaker, but it is a collaborate effort, often based on marketing tips that Rick has picked up as he drives the state. Both Rick and Padte came out of the wine distribution business, so they know how retailers think. That helps because, unlike many of the Grand Valley wineries, 75 percent of their wine sales are made to retailers instead of at the winery.

As his own distributor, Rick averages four days a week on the road. He's quite successful at marketing because you'll find Colorado Cellars wines on shelves in just about every city in the state.

The winery may be the only one in the state to offer Zinfandel, a grape that normally doesn't grow very well in Colorado, but the Turleys planted it in 1997. White Zinfandel is their number two seller, but they also have a red Zinfandel.

For all the work the Turleys put in at the winery, family life remains paramount. The winery is open every day of the week except Sundays. "I don't have much of a life outside the winery," says Rick. "So Sunday is our family day."

WINE LIST

- Alpenglo Riesling
- Cabernet Sauvignon
- Chardonnay
- Cherry
- Eclipse (sweet red)
- Estate Red
- Gewürztraminer
- Gold Rush White Port
- Merlot
- Millennium Port
- Pinot Gris
- Plum
- RoadKill Red
- Trinity Champagne
- White Zinfandel Reserve
- Zinfandel

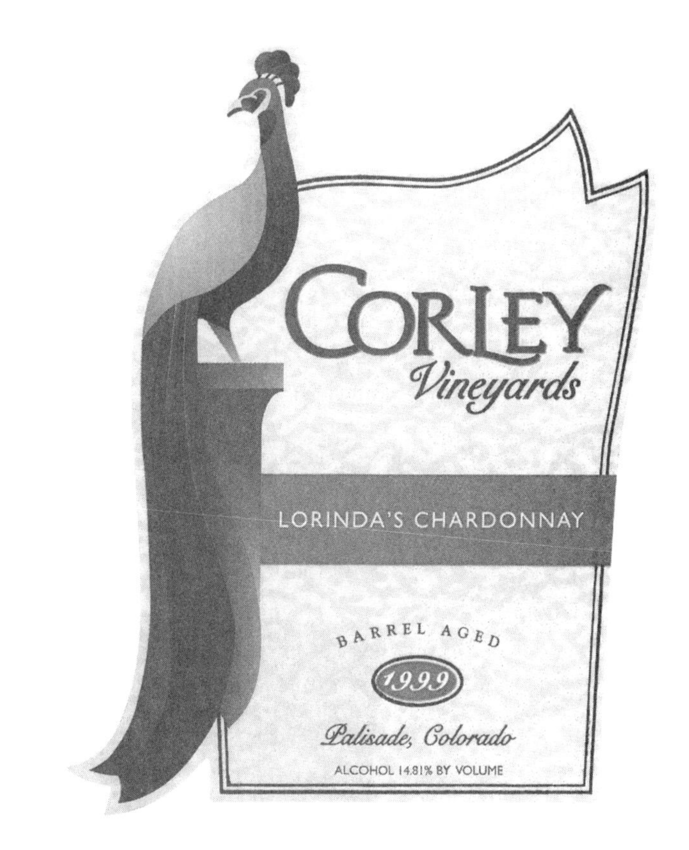

Corley Vineyards

OWNERS' NAMES: Gene and Lorinda Corley
WINEMAKER: Gene Corley
YEAR LICENSED: 1999
ADDRESS: 3820 G.25 Road, Palisade, Colorado 81526; P.O. Box 1534, Palisade, Colorado 81526 (mailing address)
TELEPHONE: 970-464-5314
WEBSITE: www.corleyvineyards.com
TASTING ROOM HOURS: By appointment only
WINE AVAILABILITY OUTSIDE WINERY: Preferred customer mailing list and selected outlets
PRICE RANGE OF WINES SOLD AT WINERY: $14.00–$22.00
WINE CLUB: Pending
ANNUAL PRODUCTION: 5,000 gallons

DIRECTIONS TO THE WINERY: From Denver, take I-70 west to Exit 44 just before it exits the canyon. Exit 44 turns into State Highway 6. Follow this for about a mile and a half to 38 road. Turn right on 38 Road and go about ¼ mile to Corley Vineyards. Look for the winery on your right at 3820 G.25 Road. From Grand Junction get off I-70 on Exit 42, which becomes Elberta Avenue, and go south to Highway 6. Left over the bridge and turn left on 38 Road.

FACILITIES AND AMENITIES: Tasting room

More than a century ago, one of the best wine grape-growing areas in Colorado was in a little triangle of flat land alongside the Colorado River near the mouth of DeBeque Canyon just east of Palisade. Back in those days the area was even called Vinelands. Those grapes, however, were ripped from the ground when Colorado passed Prohibition in 1916, and the ground was replanted with peach trees.

History took one of those "back to the future" trips near the end of the twentieth century, when peach trees were again replaced by wine grape vines in the Vinelands. Among those taking that trip were Gene and Lorinda Corley, who bought 20 acres of land in the Vinelands in 1998 after the previous owner had cut down his peach trees. That was the same year they finalized the sale of their Denver-based business and jumped feet-first into the winery business.

Gene Corley's history of wine-making doesn't reach back as far as the Vinelands era, but it is in his blood. Corley's Italian-heritage grandfather made homemade wine in southern Colorado. The wine press used by his grandfather, Frank Morelli, is on display at the Corley winery now. As a child growing up in Trinidad, Gene helped his grandfather turn that press.

The Corleys have Fess Parker, the actor-turned-winery owner, to blame for sparking their interest in getting into the wine business. It was during a trip to Parker's Santa Barbara, California, winery and nearby spa that the actor gave them a personal tour and started the Corleys wondering.

That was in the mid-1990s after the Corleys had agreed to sell their business servicing automated teller machines. Knowing that they didn't want to retire, they were looking around for other opportunities.

"We didn't even know there were Colorado wineries," Gene says. "We spent a lot of time researching land and wineries in California. We even hired a consultant out there."

The research unearthed the Colorado wine industry, and the Corleys started looking in Mesa County's Grand Valley, the state's first federally designated American Viticulture Area. They found 8 acres in the Vinelands in 1998 and planted 6 acres of Chardonnay, Merlot and Cabernet Sauvignon. Their first commercial wine in 2001, made from purchased grapes, was appropriately named "Lorinda's Chardonnay," and has the elegant peacock on the label. As a child, Lorinda used to visit a relative where she could watch peacocks on the neighboring property. Still fascinated by them, she researched and found that in some cultures they are a symbol of good luck, and that, combined with their natural elegance, would be representative of their wines.

Corley says the winery will remain a boutique enterprise, keeping its quantities low and its standard for quality high. Because the Corleys want to continue to live in the Denver area until their two sons are grown, the winery tasting room is currently open by appointment only.

If you're one of those visiting the winery, notice Lorinda's careful attention to the interior design. It makes an elegant but approachable tasting room. Instead of selling to tourists at the winery, they aim to target select groups of preferred customers. "We could get lost as a small winery," Gene says, adding that, "We may change our tune down the road."

WINE LIST

Cabernet Sauvignon
Chardonnay
Merlot

DeBeque Canyon Winery

OWNERS' NAMES: Davelyn and Bennett Price

WINEMAKER: Bennett Price

YEAR LICENSED: 1997

ADDRESS: 3943 Highway 6 and 24, Palisade, Colorado 81526; P.O. Box 1391, Palisade, Colorado 81526 (mailing address)

TELEPHONE: 970-464-0550

WEBSITE: N/A

TASTING ROOM HOURS: Friday, Saturday and Sunday 10 A.M.–5 P.M., and by appointment. Open holidays except Thanksgiving, Christmas and New Year's Day.

WINE AVAILABILITY OUTSIDE WINERY: Liquor stores, selected restaurants, mailing lists, and will ship to legal states.

PRICE RANGE OF WINES SOLD AT WINERY: $10.00–$18.00
WINE CLUB: Planned for the future
ANNUAL PRODUCTION: 2,500–3,000 gallons
DIRECTIONS TO THE WINERY: From Palisade, east of the Colorado River bridge 1.5 miles on U.S. Highways 6 and 24. From Westbound I-70, take Exit 44 and drive 1 mile west on U.S. Highway 6 and 24.
FACILITIES AND AMENITIES: Large outdoor deck for events, wine tastings, tasting and sales room as well as scenic views.

Bennett and Davy (short for Davelyn) Price are a study in tenacity and how one can overcome adversity. With a long history in many facets of the Colorado wine industry, they finally opened their own winery tasting room in 2001.

Bennett first made wine as a teenager with a friend in Arkansas from the only grapes they had, Concords. It started a life-long interest in wine and vineyards. He first moved to Denver in 1971. A geologist by trade, Bennett and his associate, Bill Stone, ordered grapes from California to make wine and continued doing that for several years. Bennett, along with many investors, had helped start Colorado Mountain Vineyards in 1978, but later sold his interest. Bennett bought an existing vineyard in 1981 in the Grand Valley, a region that had been planted to find alternative grapes. In 1983, he founded the Lone Cedar consulting company for the installation and management of his and other's vineyards. In 1986, Bennett and Davy moved to the Western Slope when the state's oil industry collapsed.

When Stephen Smith (now owner of Grande River Vineyards) moved to the Western Slope and got out of the oil business, Bennett helped him put together five parcels of land and Bennett designed and planted the vineyards in 1988.

Meanwhile Davy was on the retail side. In 1989, she helped as Doug and Sue Phillips bought the land and building for Plum Creek Cellars. Steve Smith came in as a partner and Bennett planted the vineyard. Davy managed the tasting room until 1993. She sold her interest in 1995, as she and Bennett started planning their own winery while continuing to lease vineyard property on East Orchard Mesa and make wine. Steve Rhodes of S. Rhodes Winery near Hotchkiss made his first wine from their 1996 grapes. Although Davy is a nurse at St. Mary's Hospital, she also helped Connie Strothman at Rocky Mountain Meadery with her gift shop, training the sales staff. She certainly has the hands-on background to open and run her own tasting room.

The Prices purchased property on a ridge overlooking the valley, which they named Rapid Creek Vineyard and planted Syrah and Merlot. Bennett has continued to work in other parts of the valley, designing and planting the vineyards at Canyon Wind Cellars as well as managing the vineyards for Corley Vineyards and others. The Corleys loaned the Prices space in one of their buildings to make and store their wine while the Prices finalized their arrangements for a permanent winery site.

Bennett and Davy finally opened their own winery tasting room in 2001. They'll produce several varietals and plan on their distinctive wine being a Claret, a blend of Merlot, Cabernet Sauvignon and Cabernet Franc. However, Bennett would like Syrah to be their signature wine. Unlike the Australian blended Syrahs, DeBeque's will be 100 percent Syrah. Whatever they're making, you know years of experience are behind it.

DeBeque's tasting room is in a rustic log-sided building with a deck and pots of flowers to welcome you. Notice their label, a shadow relief of DeBeque Canyon for which they're named. How appropriate that it would be designed by Tim Stone, son of Bill Stone with whom Bennett enjoyed early wine-making endeavors. Those years of experience have paid off with his own winery.

WINE LIST

Cabernet Sauvignon
Chardonnay
Claret
Merlot
Syrah
Viognier

Garfield Estates Vineyard

OWNERS' NAMES: Jeff Carr and Dave McLoughlin
WINEMAKERS: Richard Bruno and Cameron Lyeth
YEAR LICENSED: 2001
ADDRESS: 3572 G Road, Palisade, Colorado 81526
TELEPHONE: 970-464-0941
WEBSITE: www.garfieldestates.com
TASTING ROOM HOURS: Starting June 1, 2002, daily 10 A.M.–4 P.M.
WINE AVAILABILITY OUTSIDE WINERY: Not yet established
PRICE RANGE OF WINES SOLD AT WINERY: $9.00–$15.00
WINE CLUB: No
ANNUAL PRODUCTION: 5,000 gallons (est.)

DIRECTIONS TO THE WINERY: From I-70, take the Palisade Exit, 42, and take County Road 37.30 south about one mile to U.S. Highway 6 (G Road). Turn right and drive about one mile, watching for G Road to veer off to the right over the railroad tracks. Stay on G Road about 0.5 mile and look for the vineyard on the right.

FACILITIES AND AMENITIES: Tasting room in the renovated barn in the rear.

Nearly everything about the new Garfield Estates Vineyard, built on an historic peach orchard west of Palisade and licensed in 2001, speaks of California. Everything, that is, except the kinds of wines Garfield Estates wants to make.

Winery owners Jeff Carr and Dave McLoughlin are from the dot-com high-tech industry—working for Netscape Communications Corp.—and both got interested in wines and wine-making while living in northern California. They have hired two men as their winemakers, consultant Richard Bruno and Cameron Lyeth, whose roots are deep in California's wine industry. Bruno co-owns his own California winery, Vinum Cellars, while Lyeth's father started a winery in the Alexander Valley.

After Netscape was purchased by America Online Inc. in 1998, Carr and McLoughlin, who were living in the Denver area, had the money to act on their joint dream to start a winery. They looked first in California, but became attracted to Palisade, Colorado, where they found a farm near the foot of Mount Garfield, which had been in the same family for 100 years. They bought the farm and the two-story house in 2000 and immediately planted 11 acres of grapes, mostly Sauvignon Blanc and Syrah. They also have smaller quantities of Semillon, white Muscat Ottenel and Viognier. The partners decided to keep the 1910 barn behind the house, remodeling it to use as the winery and tasting room, complete with a new foundation.

Despite all the California connections, Carr and McLoughlin are intent on making premium Rhône varietal wines, figuring that would be their niche in the industry. Two of the leading grape varietals in the Northern Rhône Valley of France are Syrah for reds and Viognier for whites. Not usually found in the Rhône Valley is Sauvignon Blanc, which is often blended with Semillon, but it initially is their main white wine. It will be made in a fuller Fumé Blanc style. Carr says the Muscat Ottenel planting is experimental.

Garfield Estates made its first wine in 2000 from Syrah grapes they purchased from Grande River but only enough for personal use. They'll buy grapes from other vineyards until their own vines mature, likely in 2003.

They purchased a new Australian rotary fermentation grape press in 2001 to crush Cabernet Franc, Sauvignon Blanc and Merlot. Since those wines wouldn't be available until later in 2002, they set about making a Rosé blend from a secondary pressing of the grapes, something Carr says is common in France. The Rosé was designed to be their first commercial wine, available for the 2001 holiday season.

Carr and McLoughlin are both trained in sales and plan on being their own distributors, hopefully getting their wines in many restaurants. Years down the road where their schedules permit they also want to get more involved in making the wines.

INITIAL WINE LIST

Cabernet Franc
Fumé Blanc
Merlot
Rosé

Future

Semillon
Syrah

Grande River Vineyards

OWNER'S NAME: Stephen Smith
WINEMAKER: Stephen Smith
YEAR LICENSED: 1991
ADDRESS: 787 Elberta Avenue, Palisade, Colorado 81526; P.O. Box 129, Palisade, Colorado 81526-0129 (mailing address)
TELEPHONE: 800-COGrown (800-264-7696)
WEBSITE: www.grandriverwines.com
TASTING ROOM HOURS: Daily 9 A.M.–7 P.M. summer; 9 A.M.–6 P.M. spring and fall; 9 A.M.–5 P.M. winter
WINE AVAILABILITY OUTSIDE WINERY: Distributed through liquor stores throughout Colorado by Midwest Beverage.
PRICE RANGE OF WINES SOLD AT WINERY: $7.99–$16.99
WINE CLUB: Yes

ANNUAL PRODUCTION: 20,000 gallons

DIRECTIONS TO THE WINERY: On I-70 take Exit 42 into Palisade, turn west on the first road (Elberta) under the big sign down the long blacktop driveway to the winery.

FACILITIES AND AMENITIES: Tasting room, outdoor amphitheater with seating for up to 500 people on lawn chairs. Regular concerts from May to October (schedule on website or call).

Stephen Smith says he "just wanted a little farm" back in the 1980s when he discovered the state's fledgling wine industry badly needed grapes. Smith was getting out of the oil business, where he had been a land man, and he wanted to stay close to the earth. Grape-growing was a solid future, he figured, although he did not start making his own wine until 1986.

Now, with about 60 acres of grapes on two vineyards in the Palisade area, Smith succeeded in becoming Colorado's largest grape grower. That initial batch of wine he made in 1986 whetted an appetite that led him to open his own winery in 1991 at the foot of the distinctive Bookcliffs Ridge near Palisade. Warmth from the 2,000-foot ridge heats his vines, helping to keep them safe from winter freezes and spring frosts.

Grande River (so named because the nearby Colorado River once was named the Grand River) used to be the first winery you saw when you got off I-70 at Exit 42. That changed when St. Kathryn Cellars opened (see listing on page 50), but Grande River still is easy to get to by taking the first road west after exiting the interstate.

The winery has parking for about 250 cars on the east and south sides of the two-story 9,000-square-foot building. The large parking area accommodates not only winery visitors but also crowds who come to the winery's amphitheater for concerts on the lawn during the warm months, most of them to benefit local charities. The musical bent is toward blues, jazz and rock in recent years. Bring a picnic or get barbecue at the winery. Of course, you can buy Grande River's wines by the glass or bottle.

Heavy wood doors with a grape motif mark the entrance to the winery. Push through the doors and enter the warmth of the cathedral-ceiling tasting room and gift shop. The winery is built in the midst of about 30 acres of vineyards on a south-facing slope. The rest of the vineyards are across the Colorado River on East Orchard Mesa.

If the winery building looks like it might have been picked up by a helicopter in the Napa Valley and transplanted to the Grand

Valley, that's because Smith hired a California architect with just that in mind.

Grande River has one of the more extensive wine lists of any of the wineries in the state, with the usual ones such as Chardonnay and Merlot. It also has some other less-popular or less-familiar varietals—a Viognier and both red and white Meritage. Viognier (pronounced Vee-oh-nyay) is a delicate rare white wine that comes from the Northern Rhône Valley and entered the Napa Valley in the 1980s, where it has gradually built a small but avid following. It has a heady aroma that implies sweetness, but turns out to be dry. Perhaps two dozen wineries in the United States make it. Meritage (pronounced like "heritage") is a winemaker's word combining "merit" and "heritage" and is applied to American wines blended exclusively from Bordeaux grape varieties, either white or red. Grande River primarily uses Sauvignon Blanc and Semillon for its Meritage White, and Cabernet Sauvignon, Cabernet Franc and Merlot for the Meritage Red. Smith also has started making dessert wines such as a late harvest Semillon and a Cabernet Sauvignon Port.

Grande River continues to sell about half its grape crop every year, so you'll find its grapes in a lot of wines made by other wineries. Smith himself has helped foster the growth of the industry by offering encouragement and advice to budding winemakers. About one-third of the state's total grape production came from Grande River's vineyards in 2000. Not exactly the "little farm" Smith originally intended.

WINE LIST

Chardonnay
Desert Blush
Late Harvest Semillon
Meritage Red
Meritage White
Merlot
Port
Sauvignon Blanc
Semi Sweet
Sweet Red
Syrah
Viognier

Graystone Winery

OWNERS' NAMES: Bob and Barbara Maurer
WINEMAKER: Barbara Maurer
YEAR LICENSED: 2001
ADDRESS: 3334 F Road, Clifton, Colorado 81520
TELEPHONE: 970-523-5132
WEBSITE: To open in 2002
TASTING ROOM HOURS: By appointment only
WINE AVAILABILITY OUTSIDE WINERY: Not known at time of publication
PRICE RANGE OF WINES SOLD AT WINERY: $13.00–$25.00
WINE CLUB: No
ANNUAL PRODUCTION: 2,000–5,000 gallons

DIRECTIONS TO THE WINERY: From I-70, take the Clifton Exit and turn left at the first stop light. Go past town and approach the overpass to Palisade. As you approach, turn left (north) just before the overpass. The winery is the third left on this one-block, dead-end road. You can see the gray winery building from the top of the overpass if you overshoot your objective. If you go over the overpass on your way to Palisade, you have gone too far.

FACILITIES AND AMENITIES: Tasting room

One might say Bob and Barbara Maurer came home. They both grew up in the Palisade area and went to Mesa Junior College in Grand Junction. Bob went on to dental school and Barbara into law. But they didn't stay around, spending 25 years in Anchorage, Alaska. In fact, Bob still had his practice there while they built the winery and took many a flight to come back and work on the "farm."

"After 25 years in Alaska, I wanted a little sun," Barbara says. "We looked all over and couldn't find any place nicer than Palisade."

They bought 25 acres, and Barbara moved there in 1995. Part of their land includes a pond and wetland area with geese, quail, foxes and coyotes. They built their house first, using a poured cement and pumice mixture that matched the color of the Mancos shale on nearby Mount Garfield when it is wet; hence the name, Graystone. They thought they would plant peaches, but the wine industry was just taking off and they changed their minds, deciding to grow and sell grapes instead. They chose Pinot Gris, Pinot Blanc and Chardonnay for their niche. However, when it came time to sell, Barbara said the plants were too pretty to sell. Then Bob asked her, "Do you want a garage or a winery?" We know the answer.

In 1998 their first vineyard was ready; Barbara started taking wine-making classes and asking questions. She credits local amateur winemakers, some having made wine for 20 years, with teaching her many facets of winemaking. She enjoyed their potluck meetings and tips from Scott Miller who owns the Lil' Ole' Winemaker store in Grand Junction.

One need only to talk to Barbara for a few minutes to feel her contagious enthusiasm for growing grapes and making wine. It's easy to see why she thinks everyone in the Colorado wine industry is so helpful. Who could have resisted her quick smile and thirst for knowledge? This passion can be seen in the Maurers' son, Casper, who is in the midst of dental school but leaning toward becoming a winemaker. In fact, while other kids home from school might take life easy, he chose to train vines.

The future holds an expansion of the vineyard with red grapes and Lawrence pear trees, the opening of the tasting room with an antique bar, developing a sparkling white wine in the Italian style, but staying small enough to "visit these grapes every day."

"I want to bring the varietal through into the bottle," Barbara says. "I believe in vineyard management." They use all handpicking and soft, whole-cluster pressing in their new press from Germany. The Maurers are completely geared to produce quality wines.

WINE LIST

Chardonnay
Pinot Blanc
Pinot Gris
Vintage Port

Plum Creek Cellars

OWNERS' NAMES: Doug and Sue Phillips
WINEMAKER: Jenne Baldwin
YEAR LICENSED: 1984
ADDRESS: 3708 G Road, Palisade, Colorado 81526
TELEPHONE: 970-464-7586
WEBSITE: N/A
TASTING ROOM HOURS: Open 7 days a week, 9:30 A.M.–6 P.M. April through November; 10 A.M.–5 P.M. December through March
WINE AVAILABILITY OUTSIDE WINERY: At most liquor shops and some restaurants in Colorado. Will ship to legal states. Also, can be tasted at Tewskbury & Co., 1512 Larimer Street, Writer's Square, in downtown Denver.
PRICE RANGE OF WINES SOLD AT WINERY: $5.99–$20.99

WINE CLUB: No

ANNUAL PRODUCTION: 18,000–30,000 gallons (est.)

DIRECTIONS TO THE WINERY: From I-70, take Exit 42 at Palisade. Travel south to G Road (Old U.S. Highways 6 and 24). At G Road go west 0.25 mile and the winery is on the north (right).

FACILITIES AND AMENITIES: Tasting room filled with fine art and antiques with seating by a large stone fireplace, picnic area on landscaped grounds, shaded patio area.

As young as Colorado's wine industry is, it becomes difficult to call any winery the "gray hair" or respected elder. But if any winery occupies that position, it is Plum Creek Cellars. The designation is partly due to the fact that Plum Creek is the third oldest winery in the state, licensed in 1984, but also because year-in and year-out Doug and Sue Phillips have worked to raise the quality and gain recognition for the industry as a whole. The old "rising tides lifts all boats" philosophy applies to these tireless advocates of Colorado wine.

Even though they spend a lot of their time as attorneys in Denver, you can find the Phillipses frequently at their winery on the weekend, where they help pour wine and give tours of their new winery building. We've seen Doug out in the vineyards explaining viticulture to a tourist.

Although nearly 20 years old, Plum Creek Cellars has a large "great room" tasting room built in 1998. With its large fireplace and comfy couches, it has the feel of a well-stocked mountain chalet. The tasting room is large enough for a sit-down dinner for seventy-five people.

As you drive into their parking lot, notice the 1,200-pound "Chardonnay Chicken" metal sculpture by local sculptor Lyle Nichols. On the east side of the winery is a clematis-draped pergola with chairs and tables to sit and enjoy the afternoon. Don't try to move the solid iron furniture—one of the benches weighs 380 pounds.

Plum Creek gets grapes from its Palisade vineyard and the larger Redstone vineyard in Delta County. The Redstone vineyard annually produces about two-thirds of the state's Chardonnays (although a freeze and frost in 1999 and 2000 damaged the crops) and is reputed to be the world's highest Chardonnay vineyard.

"That's one of the dangers of planting Chardonnay at 6,000 feet," says Doug, a former Green Beret captain. "There's always the danger of late frosts. But when it's good, it is great."

As good as Plum Creek's Chardonnay is, the winery's top seller is the reserve Merlot. That's a varietal that Doug believes eventually could be Colorado's signature wine, much like Pinot Noir is the signature of the Oregon wine industry. If it isn't Merlot, the choice would be Cabernet Sauvignon, he says, although Sue believes Cabernet Franc and Sangiovese are more distinctively Colorado.

Plum Creek has been making a well-received Sangiovese, the principal grape in Italian Chianti, since the mid-1990s. Sometimes Doug and winemaker Jenne Baldwin turn it into a dessert wine because of the qualities of the grape. Baldwin took over as winemaker in the late 1990s due to the illness of Plum Creek's founding winemaker, Eric Brunner, who was a mentor for many budding oenologists in the Grand Valley.

You might be wondering where Plum Creek got its name. The name is derived from the Plum Creek that flows close to the foothills south of Denver in Douglas County, a location originally considered for the winery. That idea was given up because it would have meant shipping the grapes from the Western Slope every year.

WINE LIST

Carlson's Cherry Wine
Chardonnay
Merlot
Palisade Red
Palisade Rosé
Reserve Cabernet Sauvignon
Reserve Merlot
Riesling
Riesling Ice Wine

Rocky Mountain Meadery

OWNERS' NAMES: Fred and Connie Strothman
WINEMAKER: Fred Strothman
YEAR LICENSED: 1995
ADDRESS: 3701 G Road, Palisade, Colorado 81526
TELEPHONE: 970-464-7899
WEBSITE: www.wic.net/meadery
TASTING ROOM HOURS: 10 A.M.–5 P.M. daily
WINE AVAILABILITY OUTSIDE WINERY: Distributed by Pinnacle Distributing Co. outside of Mesa County and throughout Colorado. Ship to legal states.
PRICE RANGE OF WINES SOLD AT WINERY: $8.95–$15.95

WINE CLUB: No

ANNUAL PRODUCTION IN GALLONS: N/A

DIRECTIONS TO THE WINERY: Take I-70 to Exit 42. Turn right on Elberta Road and travel about 1 mile to G Road (U.S. 6); travel west about one-quarter mile. On the left (south) side of the road look for the gazebo and the Meadery building.

FACILITIES AND AMENITIES: Gazebo available for picnics and parties, tasting room, gift shop featuring wine-related items and gourmet foods, ample parking, restrooms and views of the Grand Mesa and Mt. Garfield, vineyard and orchard for strolling.

When retired Denver Federal Administrative Judge Fred Strothman set out in 1995 to make mead, the fabled elixir of the ancients so popular that it permeates several Shakespearean plays, he almost had to reinvent the drink himself. At the time, few places in the United States made mead, and Strothman had to do a lot of research to find out how it is made.

The basic facts were not difficult to come by because mead's ingredients are few: honey, water and yeast. Beyond that, mead offers a lot of tinkering. Sometimes acid is added to balance the sweetness. The French style of mead often uses fruit or fruit juice. Since the mix all depends on honey, one can experiment with various kinds of honey that bees produce.

Strothman became a master of mead. Whether or not his success spawned an industry could be debated, but there is now an association of mead makers, and the number of meaderies has blossomed across the country. Maybe Strothman was on the leading edge of a resurging interest in the product. But back in the Elizabethan days of Shakespeare it appeared to be the drink of choice in English roadhouses. Indeed, one of the Bard's most lasting characters, the rogue Falstaff, seemed to live on a mead variety called Sack.

Strothman won't tell you all his secrets, but he makes great batches of mead to fit a variety of palates. Most people consider mead to be sweet, and it often is, but the Rocky Mountain Meadery makes a very dry mead called King Arthur that smells of honey but without the sugar taste. The basic meads are named after King Arthur's court, with Lancelot a medium dry, Guinevere semi-sweet and Camelot, the sweetest of all.

There also are meads flavored with fruit wines: peach, blackberry, raspberry, apricot and cherry. Strothman makes the fruit wines separately and then blends them to his satisfaction with the mead. He also makes a hard cider from local apples and pears.

Strothman buys honey in 5,000-gallon batches, blending it with water and yeast in 55-gallon dairy tanks for fermentation. It takes about 25 days to ferment, depending on the sweetness desired, and then is ready for bottling.

"It's a very labor-intensive process," Strothman says.

The mead-making occurs in the rear of a 5,000 square-foot steel building the Strothmans built in 1995, which is used also to make the wines sold under the St. Kathryn Cellars label, which the Strothmans also own (see separate St. Kathryn listing).

When you step in the front door of the Meadery, which is sheltered by several large trees, you're in Connie Strothman's charming empire, a 1,500-square-foot tasting room and gift shop that feels like home the minute the door shuts behind you. Those double doors at the entrance were saved from one of the couple's former homes. Lace curtains cover the windows and the displays invite inspection. The centerpiece of the tasting room is a black walnut counter, made from a piece of wood the Strothmans had been carting around with them for 30 years.

All the items in the store have a fruit, wine or honey connection and most are from Colorado. Sign your name to their mailing list and Connie will ship you one of her periodic newsletters, which usually has several recipes using their meads.

WINE LIST

Traditional Meads

Camelot
Guinevere
King Arthur
Lancelot

Fruit and Honey Blended Meads

Apricots 'n Honey
Blackberry 'n Honey
Cherry 'n Honey
Peaches 'n Honey
Raspberry 'n Honey

Cider (hard)

Apple Cider
Pear Cider

St. Kathryn Cellars

OWNERS' NAMES: Fred and Connie Strothman
WINEMAKER: Fred Strothman
YEAR LICENSED: 1995
ADDRESS: 785 Elberta Avenue, Palisade, Colorado 81526
TELEPHONE: 970-464-9288
WEBSITE: www.st-kathryn-cellars.com
TASTING ROOM HOURS: Daily 10 A.M.–5 P.M.; summers 9:30 A.M.–7 P.M.
WINE AVAILABILITY OUTSIDE WINERY: Local liquor stores only but will ship to legal states.
PRICE RANGE OF WINES SOLD AT WINERY: $8.95–$21.95
WINE CLUB: No
ANNUAL PRODUCTION IN GALLONS: N/A
DIRECTIONS TO THE WINERY: From I-70, take Exit 42 at Palisade and the yellow winery and events center is the first building you reach on the west side of the road.

FACILITIES AND AMENITIES: This was built as an events center as well as a tasting room and gift shop, with ample parking and indoor seating for 200 people, with a picnic area and patio.

You see a big yellow house with a tower as soon as you get off I-70 at Palisade. When you open the front door and walk in, there on the foyer wall is a photograph of Fred Strothman's mother, the woman who has given her name, Kathryn, to this distinctive winery. Strothman says he named the winery after his mother because, just before she died, she said she would watch over the winery from heaven. In addition to naming the winery after her, her photo is also on the wine labels.

Strothman opened the facility in August of 1999, although it had been licensed much earlier under the Confre Cellars umbrella corporation, which also is over the Rocky Mountain Meadery (see previous listing) and Rocky Mountain Cidery labels.

St. Kathryn Cellars has everything in place to produce wine, but all the wine made under its label has been made at Strothman's nearby meadery operation. The facility still has much to offer visitors with its 4,500-square-foot tasting room/gift shop as well as an events center complete with a commercial catering kitchen. Strothman says he may eventually make wine at St. Kathryn, but initially it was more cost effective to keep everything under one roof.

Just as at the Rocky Mountain Meadery, Connie Strothman oversees the gift shop at St. Kathryn. It is filled with wine-related and Colorado gifts. The gift items may appeal more to women than men, but that's by design because the center honors a woman, says Jane Fine Foster, who is St. Kathryn Cellar's chief executive officer.

The portion of the building that is the events center was originally a peach packing shed, but you can't tell that from a glance. The 4,000-square-foot facility has been completely renovated, including an acoustic ceiling treatment to help the sound effects. The building is used for weddings and other large functions, including many charitable events. Foster says they have handled as many as 330 people with tents set up outside.

Strothman makes more than a dozen kinds of wine—everything from traditional Chardonnay from Colorado grapes to fruit wines. The winery's signature wine, he says, is an off-dry fruit wine called Blueberry Bliss. He brags that between St. Kathryn and Rocky Mountain Meadery he is the biggest producer in the state, but he declines to say how much wine and mead that might be.

In the year 2000 Strothman says he harvested 8 tons of grapes to the acre from his vineyards, which is nearly double what most other growers produce. Some growers and winemakers prune back the grape bunches on the vines, arguing that fewer grapes provide more intense flavor, but Strothman believes this is unnecessary.

As you leave St. Kathryn Cellars, there is a wall map of the world that shows the kind of drawing power the facility has. There are pins, signifying the hometowns of visitors, from places like Kazakhstan, Nepal and Armenia. Strothman has certainly put Palisade on the map.

WINE LIST

Apple Blossom
Blueberry Bliss
Cameo Rose
Chardonnay
Chardonnay Reserve
Cranberry Kiss
Golden Pear
Merlot
Merlot Port
Merlot Reserve
Ruby Red
Strawberry-Rhubarb
White Merlot

Two Rivers Winery

OWNERS' NAMES: Robert and Billie Witham
WINEMAKER: Glenn Foster
YEAR LICENSED: 1999
ADDRESS: 2087 Broadway, Grand Junction, Colorado 81503
TELEPHONE: 970-255-1471
WEBSITE: www.tworiverswinery.com
TASTING ROOM HOURS: 10:30 A.M.–6 P.M. Monday–Saturday; 12 P.M.–5 P.M. Sunday
WINE AVAILABILITY OUTSIDE WINERY: Available in major liquor stores in large population areas and resorts. Some restaurants, principally in the Grand Junction area.
PRICE RANGE OF WINES SOLD AT WINERY: $11.50–$13.25
WINE CLUB: In development

ANNUAL PRODUCTION: 19,000 gallons

DIRECTIONS TO THE WINERY: From the east, take I-70 to Redlands Parkway/24 Road Exit. Take Redlands Parkway south (left) about 2.5 miles to the second stop light (Broadway/Colorado Highway 340). Turn right (west) onto Broadway for 2.25 miles to the winery on the south side of the highway. From the west, take I-70 to Fruita/Highway 340 Exit; take Highway 340 east about 5 miles and the winery is on the south (right) side of the highway.

FACILITIES AND AMENITIES: Tasting room, front terrace and fermentation room available for intimate catered dinner parties and events. Large outdoor Chateau Deux Fleuves Vineyard Pavilion has spectacular views and landscaped grounds for larger groups. In late 2001, they began contruction on a 13,000-square-foot conference center/bed-and-breakfast/ indoor events center.

The Two Rivers Winery in Grand Junction is about as close to a winery in France as one can get in Colorado. The stone building that houses the winery looks as if it had been snatched from Bordeaux and plopped down in the midst of an 11-acre vineyard near the confluence of the Colorado and Gunnison Rivers.

That French theme is evidenced not only on the outside of the building, but also in the tasting room, the fermentation and storage rooms and in the name of the winery's vineyard, "Chateau Deux Fleuves."

Walk through the massive wood entrance door and into a tasting room that feels like a hunting lodge with the imposing flagstone fireplace and wood floor. Notice the painting of the attractive woman over the fireplace mantel and the title underneath: "Ask Me and I'll Say Yes," which seems to encourage adventure and exploration.

This is a winery where you'll definitely want to take a tour. The walls of the fermentation room are covered with *trompe l'oeil* French country murals. Through interior windows you can see the barrel storage room.

Witham, who opened the winery in late 1999, is aiming for French-style wines that are friendly to the palate. He plans on sticking with four varietals—Riesling, Chardonnay, Cabernet Sauvignon and Merlot; all but the Riesling are planted in the vineyards. His first releases were made from Colorado grapes he purchased, since his own vines were not yet producing. He harvested his first grapes in 2001, with the wines expected to be released in 2003.

The winemaker at Two Rivers is Glenn Foster, whose father founded the Ravenswood Winery in California. Foster's wife is from Colorado and enticed him to move to Colorado's wine region.

Both Withams are Colorado natives, Bob from Craig and Billie from Meeker, and they have known each other since high school. After serving as a military policeman in Vietnam, Bob received his degree in criminology but couldn't find a job. He started as a nursing home administrator in Steamboat Springs, moving up to president of the company, which operated 280 nursing homes around the country. He left the company after an initial public offering, started his own Austin, Texas, company developing retirement communities and eventually sold that. Billie, an accountant and Medicare consultant, was executive director of the Austin retirement community.

"We moved to Grand Junction and discovered that they had a wine industry," Witham says. "We started studying it, treating it like a master's thesis, and got comfortable with the idea we could do it."

Two Rivers is some 20 miles from any other Grand Valley winery, which is one of the reasons the Withams are making it into a destination stop with the new events center and bed-and-breakfast. Upon completion, it will contain a twenty-five-person boardroom with a wine bar and event seating for about 150 people. There will also be a catering kitchen and a breakfast room overlooking an upstairs balcony. The B&B area upstairs was designed for nine rooms priced in the $85–$140 range.

WINE LIST

Cabernet Sauvignon
Chardonnay
Merlot
Riesling

WITHOUT TASTING ROOMS

Reeder Mesa Vineyards

OWNERS' NAMES: Doug and Kris Vogel
WINEMAKER: Doug Vogel
YEAR LICENSED: 2000
ADDRESS: 7799 Reeder Mesa Road, Whitewater, Colorado 81527-9510
TELEPHONE: 970-242-7468
WEBSITE: N/A
TASTINGS: In the future
WINE AVAILABILITY OUTSIDE WINERY: Limited to local festivals

PRICE RANGE OF WINES SOLD AT WINERY: $10.00–$12.00
WINE CLUB: No
ANNUAL PRODUCTION: 400 gallons, increasing annually as vineyard matures
DIRECTIONS TO THE WINERY: N/A
FACILITIES AND AMENITIES: Future plans for a tasting room.

A few miles southeast of Grand Junction, Doug and Kris Vogel's home, vineyard and winery sit atop 5,600-foot Reeder Mesa with a 360-degree view. Doug is a mechanic and Kris is a graphic artist, but they looked around the Grand Valley and saw others raising grapes, which led them to plant their own Riesling grapes in 1994.

"We weren't going to be a winery," says Doug. "We just started making it and we'd give it away to friends and they just loved it, so we decided to make more and get licensed." They chose Riesling because they heard the vines were the most winter-hardy, and the wine's a favorite of theirs.

When asked how they learned, they told us they learned from books, the Vintner's Association, some classes and tips from consultants hired by the Colorado Wine Industry Development Board. One consultant suggested different yeasts, tests and fining. The couple is a good example of how you can teach yourself. They are thinking of taking some on-line courses to learn more. Now the Vogels, with the help of some friends, do all the picking, vine-training, pruning, and any other vineyard management job that needs to be done. Kris, of course, designed their attractive label.

The near future includes selling Riesling and Chenin Blanc at festivals beginning in 2002. Later, even more changes may happen. "We're trying to get the vineyard established and see how much we're producing," Doug says. "I've been a mechanic all my life, but I'd like to get out of it."

WINE LIST

Chenin Blanc
Riesling

ACCOMMODATIONS AND DINING

PALISADE BED-AND-BREAKFASTS

BEWELCOME BED-AND-BREAKFAST

649 Aldrea Vista Court
Palisade, Colorado 81526
970-464-0884
Hosts: Jim and Joy Seckle
A pleasant home on a mesa, looking across the Grand Valley with three rooms; full breakfasts.

THE GARDEN HOUSE

3587 G Road
Palisade, Colorado 81526
970-464-4686 or 1-800-305-4686
Hosts: Joyce and Bill Haas
Enjoy full breakfasts in the dining room; they have four rooms in a big house, but you may prefer one of the three in the back part of the house for more solitude. Joyce offers an array of changing breakfasts, self-help beverages and, sometimes, homemade cookies.

HUBERT'S PLACE

507 35½ Road
Palisade, Colorado 81526
970-464-5981 or 1-888-355-2363
Hostess: Linda Mowrer
Up on East Orchard Mesa (near Carlson's Vineyards) is a charming little house named for the man who lived there most of his life with his family. This is total privacy, a 1,000-square-foot home that's all yours with two bedrooms, kitchen, living room, dining room and landscaped yard. Linda provides beverages and some snacks in the kitchen and delivers your cooked breakfast when you want it (her home sits in the back).

MT. GARFIELD BED-AND-BREAKFAST

3355 F Road
Clifton, Colorado 81520
970-434-8120 or 1-800-547-9108
Hosts: Todd and Carrie McKay
Website: www.gj.net/mckayinn

Just a little drive down F Road in a peach orchard is a large home with four rooms, hot tub and swimming pool; full breakfasts. Their sign can be misleading; Todd is also a realtor.

THE ORCHARD HOUSE

3573 E½ Road
Palisade, Colorado 81526
970-464-0529
Hostess: Stephanie Schmid

This 4,000 square-foot home with a wrap-around porch, an orchard, a generous-sized living room for guests, and views across the mesa has four large rooms, full breakfasts, and peace and quiet on East Orchard Mesa.

PEARADICE FARM

629 35 Road
P.O. Box 14
Palisade, Colorado 81526
970-464-5751
Hosts: Jackie and Frank Davidson

Just two miles west of the town of Palisade is an 1896 farmhouse set on 6 acres, restored by Frank. Behind it is the carriage house (B&B) with living room, full kitchen, a brass queen bed in the bedroom, small yard and private patio. While Jackie doesn't cook your breakfast, she provides colorful fresh eggs from her chickens, biscotti, coffee and creamers. A complete getaway.

THE VINEYARDS VICTORIAN

398 West 1st Street
Palisade, Colorado 81526
970-464-4942
Website: www.vineyards-victorian.com

Historic home in the town of Palisade with two large rooms decorated in wine-country colors with either a private steam room or two-person soaker tub. Your choice of full breakfasts in the dining room on the weekends or they pay for your breakfast in a local restaurant during the week.

PALISADE

CASTLE ROCK LODGE

3939 Highways 6 & 24
Palisade, Colorado 81526
970-464-7117

Remodeled motel with six themed rooms and an outdoor hot tub. Located next door to DeBeque Winery.

GRAND JUNCTION

LOS ALTOS BED-AND-BREAKFAST

375 Hillview Drive
Grand Junction, Colorado 81503
970-256-0694 or 1-888-774-0982
Hosts: Lee and Young-Ja Garrett

Built on a hilltop with expansive views, this B&B has six rooms, some with decks; serves a full breakfast in the formal dining room and tea at 4 P.M.

DINING IN THE GRAND VALLEY

PALISADE

THE TEAPOT COTTAGE

336 Main Street
Palisade, Colorado 81526
970-464-6400

Enjoy lunch (changes daily), just a "cuppa" of the many teas or shop for tea-related gifts for sale surrounding the tables.

GRAND JUNCTION

CHEF'S

936 North Avenue
Grand Junction, Colorado 81501-2413
970-243-9673
Website: www.gjchefs.com

On Winefest weekend this has been the site for one of the Friday night Winemakers' dinners, pairing a Colorado wine with each course. During the rest of the year, you can enjoy New World cuisine and pick wine from a well-chosen wine list Tuesday–Saturday, 5 p.m–9 P.M. The chef is creative and uses fresh local produce.

CRYSTAL CAFÉ AND BAKE SHOP

314 Main Street
Grand Junction, Colorado 81501-2413
970-242-8843

The locals know the spot for breakfast and lunch, Monday–Friday, 7 A.M.–1:45 P.M. and Saturday, 8 A.M.–12 P.M. You can have freshly made pastries or full breakfasts and buy something to take home from their bakery.

IL BISTRO ITALIAN

400 Main Street
Grand Junction, Colorado 81501-2413
970-243-8622

A bistro in the middle of the desert with a chef whose origins are Northern Italy and who brings that authenticity to his cooking. Open Monday 11 A.M.–2 P.M. and 11 A.M.–9 P.M., Tuesday–Saturday.

ROCKSLIDE BREW PUB

401 Main Street
Grand Junction, Colorado 81501-2413
970-245-2111

It is a brewery, but the pub serves Colorado wine and decent pub food with TVs to catch your favorite game. Open 11 A.M.–midnight daily with Sunday brunch at 8 A.M.

WW PEPPERS

753 Horizon Court
Grand Junction, Colorado 81501-2413
970-245-9251

This is a favorite of some winemakers for its relaxed atmosphere, southwestern fare, steaks and seafood. Open 11 A.M.–2 P.M. for lunch; 4:30 P.M.–9 P.M. Monday–Friday for dinner; 5 P.M.–9 P.M. Saturday and Sunday.

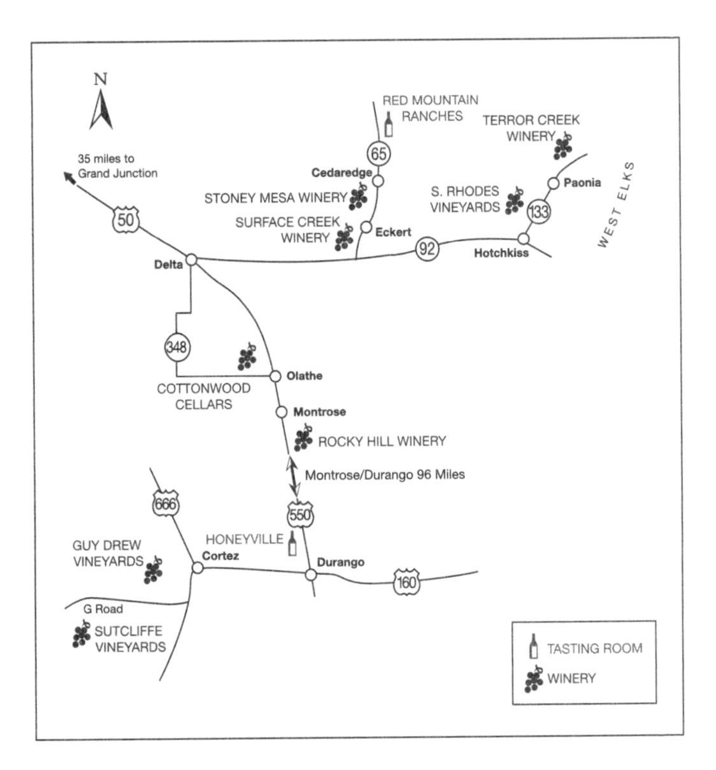
N
35 miles to
Grand Junction
RED MOUNTAIN
RANCHES
TERROR CREEK
WINERY
65
Cedaredge
STONEY MESA WINERY
S. RHODES
VINEYARDS
Paonia
WEST ELKS
133
SURFACE CREEK
WINERY
Eckert
50
92
Hotchkiss
Delta
348
COTTONWOOD
CELLARS
Olathe
Montrose
ROCKY HILL WINERY
Montrose/Durango 96 Miles
666
550
HONEYVILLE
GUY DREW
VINEYARDS
Cortez
Durango
160
G Road
SUTCLIFFE
VINEYARDS
TASTING ROOM
WINERY

DELTA AND MONTROSE COUNTIES AND SOUTHWEST WINERIES

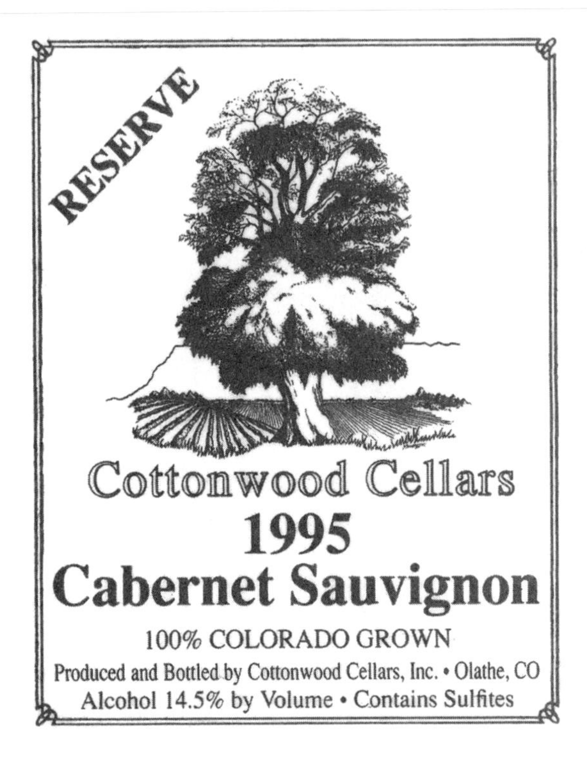

Cottonwood Cellars

OWNERS' NAMES: Keith and Diana Read
WINEMAKER: Keith Read
YEAR LICENSED: 1994
ADDRESS: 5482 Highway 348, Olathe, Colorado 81425; P.O. Box 940, Olathe, Colorado 81425 (mailing address)
TELEPHONE: 970-323-6224
WEBSITE: www.cottonwoodcellars.com
TASTING ROOM HOURS: Wednesday through Sunday, 11 A.M.–6 P.M., July through September or by appointment. Check website for special tastings and information on events.
WINE AVAILABILITY OUTSIDE WINERY: Will ship to legal states and consult their website for liquor store and restaurant listings.
PRICE RANGE OF WINES SOLD AT WINERY: $6.99–$28.00
WINE CLUB: One is planned; see website.
ANNUAL PRODUCTION: 5,000 gallons

DIRECTIONS TO THE WINERY: Take U.S. Highway 50 to Olathe. At the signal light turn west on Colorado Highway 348; continue for 3.4 miles. Cottonwood Cellars will be on your right.

FACILITIES AND AMENITIES: Large tasting room; picnic under the cottonwood in the front yard. Check website for events, dinners, and so on.

Diana and Keith Read are no longer gazing over their farm in Olathe, Colorado, as a take-it-easy retirement spot. That was the original intention in 1993 when they decided to leave their computer-related jobs in California. But Keith thought he might want to plant some crops on his 52 acres in western Colorado. He attended a Colorado State University alfalfa conference and at the luncheon heard a speech about growing grapes in Colorado. That did it! There's been no looking back for the Reads since.

Diana and Keith had always enjoyed good wine and decided to "make wines we like to drink. By doing that we find other people like them as well," Diana says. They work with chefs in wine and food competitions and have found their wines well received since their winery opened in 1994.

They planted 10 acres in 1995, and in 1998 they started construction on a new building with a tasting room. From one small building housing everything, they have built the new facility, including a large tasting room and a storage room with a 5,000-gallon capacity and the potential to hold 200 oak barrels for aging.

Planting grapes was almost unheard of in this farm/ranch section of Colorado, and the Reads were scoffed at by neighbors when they took off top soil to reach the rocky subsoil grape vines would love. Locals now see them as a benefit to the region. They planted 14 additional acres in 2000 and 2001. There was so much work that they talked Keith's brother, Richard, into moving to the farm and becoming their vineyard manager.

"We're trying to develop a French Chateau winery," Diana says. "You grow grapes and make wines that you can lay down several years. It's becoming a lost art. Three generations...the first one plants the grapes, the second ones makes the wine, the third one grows the business." Now one of her sons is interested in helping.

They do slow fermentation with an emphasis on quality. Diana says they want to improve the wines each time they make them. If this makes Diana and Keith sound like wine snobs, you only have to walk through the beautiful mahogany doors and into the tasting room filled with antiques to be greeted by a woman with long black hair (Diana), and her quick smile will dispel that impression. While she's pouring, she'll be talking and laughing a mile a minute.

The winery is off the beaten path, but she says once the "The Ride the Rockies" bicycle tour came by and riders stopped to buy wine. She later delivered the wine to their motel room. That must have seemed like nothing compared to the thirty to forty cases they deliver to the Front Range every two weeks in their temperature-controlled truck. They handle all their own shipping and distribution. Says Diana, "We learn more about our customers than if we went through a distributor."

There is a spot for a picnic under the big old cottonwood outside. Then take the memory of the setting home. It's pictured on their main Cottonwood Cellars label in a pen-and-ink drawing by local artist, Diana Robertson. They also make wine under two other labels, Olathe Winery and Anthony's.

WINE LIST

Cottonwood Cellars label

Cabernet Sauvignon
Carneros Chardonnay
Edna Valley Chardonnay
Merlot
Pinot Noir
Reserve Cabernet Sauvignon

Olathe Winery label

Claret
Dry Gewürztraminer
Gewürztraminer
Johannesburg Riesling
Lemberger
Rose of Cabernet

Anthony's label

Colorado Merlot

Guy Drew Vineyards

OWNERS' NAMES: Ruth and Guy Drew
WINEMAKER: Guy Drew
YEAR LICENSED: 2000
ADDRESS: 20057 Road G, Cortez, Colorado 81321; P.O. Box 1750, Cortez, Colorado 81321 (mailing address)
TELEPHONE: 970-565-4958
WEBSITE: N/A
TASTING ROOM HOURS: By appointment
WINE AVAILABILITY OUTSIDE WINERY: Only at winery
PRICE RANGE OF WINES SOLD AT WINERY: $10.00–$12.50
WINE CLUB: Yes
ANNUAL PRODUCTION: 2,200 gallons
DIRECTIONS TO THE WINERY: South of Cortez, Colorado, 4.2 miles West on G Road (Airport Rd.) from U.S. 666
FACILITIES AND AMENITIES: In development.

Leaving the "rat race" in the big city for a scenic piece of land that could produce your livelihood is the yearning of many, but Guy and Ruth Drew did it. In Denver Guy had been involved in industrial equipment and Ruth was a paralegal and in sales. They moved to McElmo Canyon near Cortez and when asked if they had ever made wine before, we were surprised when they said no. They made their first wine, a Cabernet Franc for personal consumption, in 1999 from grapes they purchased in Colorado.

Out of that first experience a desire to make quality wine grew. And it started with planting grapes, and not in a half-hearted fashion. They have 11 acres in vineyards near their home, 9 acres 14 miles down McElmo Canyon, and another 13 acres nearby. Not only do they have numerous acres, but they also have planted 11 different varietals, including the five Bordeaux reds—Cabernet Sauvignon, Merlot, Cabernet Franc, Malbec, Petit Verdot—plus Syrah. The whites are Riesling, Chardonnay, Sauvignon Blanc, Viognier and Semillon.

Guy is not sure how many of his wines will be blends or varietals (varietals are predominantly one grape). He says it will depend on the grapes. The first releases under their Crooked Creek Cellars label will be blends, a red and a white table wine.

Ruth, who Guy says is the "real boss," can be found doing many jobs: working in the vineyard, training vines, working in her formal gardens or with the organic vegetables they grow to sell at farmers' markets in Cortez and Dolores.

You wouldn't say they're going to expand exponentially, but from 400 cases in 2001, they plan to "ramp up" to 7,500 cases, possibly by 2004. Referring to the future, Guy says, "I hope by that time I can afford a winemaker."

If all this doesn't seem like enough to do, Guy was appointed by Governor Bill Owens to serve two years on the Colorado Wine Industry Development Board, beginning 2001. The Drews may have left "the rat race," but they certainly aren't shirking work.

If you're like us, you may think you have traveled all over Colorado, but discovering McElmo Canyon was a delight for us. In addition, by visiting the Drews you'll also see a number of Anasazi archaeological sites scattered throughout their vineyards.

INITIAL WINE LIST

Table Red
Table White

Rocky Hill Winery

OWNERS' NAMES: Marschall and David Fansler
WINEMAKER: David Fansler
YEAR LICENSED: 1993
ADDRESS: 18380 U.S. Highway 550, Montrose, Colorado 81401 (plan to move the winery by fall 2002 to the Grand Valley, 221 31 3/10 Road, on Orchard Mesa south of Grand Junction)
TELEPHONE: 970-249-3765 (subject to winery relocation)
WEBSITE: www.rockyhillwinery.com
TASTING ROOM HOURS: 10 A.M.–6 P.M., Monday–Saturday.
WINE AVAILABILITY OUTSIDE WINERY: At major liquor stores in Colorado. Also will ship to legal states.

PRICE RANGE OF WINES SOLD AT WINERY: $7.00–$14.00
WINE CLUB: No
ANNUAL PRODUCTION: 2,000 gallons
DIRECTIONS TO THE WINERY: South of Montrose on U.S. Highway 550 about two miles on the east side of the highway. The winery plans to move to the Grand Valley area by fall 2002 (see address above). The website should have updated information on the relocation.
FACILITIES AND AMENITIES: Picnic area under cottonwood trees next to a stream, with views of the San Juan Mountains.

Dave Fansler, the owner and winemaker at Rocky Hill Winery, is one of those people whose good nature and self-deprecating humor is infectious. He readily calls himself a "mad scientist," gives fun names to some of his products, and seems to be laughing and smiling all the time.

"Some wineries like to be traditional," he says. "Not me. I like to try new things." You'll see some varietal names on Fansler's wine list you'll recognize. But there also are a Ski Bunny Blush, San Juan Gold, Montrose and Black Canyon. The latter is a dry red blend of Cabernet Franc and Merlot, but with a taste distinctly its own.

Rocky Hill is a winery in a state of transition. When we wrote our first edition in 1997, the winery was located in a former A&W root beer stand just south of Montrose's downtown. Fansler sold that property and moved the winery about two miles south on U.S. Highway 550. He brought along a mural from the first winery, depicting German maidens stomping grapes, which is now part of an interior wall.

By late summer 2001, Fansler was talking about moving the winery again—this time to an 8-acre piece of land he owns on Orchard Mesa near Grand Junction. Among the grapes he has planted there are Riesling, Muscat, Chenin Blanc, Gewürztraminer and Cabernet Sauvignon. Construction on the new winery was expected to be completed by fall of 2002; check his website or call for the exact opening.

Fansler's most popular wine may be one made from Olathe pie and Bing cherries. He ferments the cherries with their skins on, presses the juice when the fermentation stops and then says he throws the lees (skins, seeds and stems) into the fields for the deer to eat. The deer eat the lees like candy, Fansler says, even getting tipsy on the remaining alcohol.

Some of the cherries are used in a cherry Merlot blend Fansler calls Ouray. Another unique blend is his Riesling Noir, a combination of Riesling and Merlot grapes. You're never quite sure what new blend you'll be getting at Rocky Hill. Another example are Chardonnays from three recent vintages, one fermented "sur lees" (with the skins, stems and seeds), one using American yeast and aged in oak, and another with French yeast and oak.

Rocky Hill also has cut back its production by about half of what it was in the mid-1990s because Fansler has started to focus on other interests such as golf, scuba diving and travel. Fansler was married in the summer of 2001 to Marschall, who says she is very interested in helping him with the wine business.

WINE LIST

Black Canyon (Merlot/Cabernet blend)
Chardonnay
Chenin Blanc
Cherry
Gewürztraminer
Montrose (Beaujolais-style red)
Ouray (cherry/Merlot blend)
Red Mountain Merlot
Riesling Noir (Riesling/Merlot blend)
San Juan Gold (sweet white)
Sauvignon Blanc
Ski Bunny Blush (semisweet rosé)

Stoney Mesa Winery

OWNERS' NAMES: Ron Neal, Donna Neal, Bret Neal
WINEMAKER: Bret Neal
YEAR LICENSED: 1993
ADDRESS: 1619 2125 Drive, Cedaredge, Colorado 81413; P.O. Box 966, Cedaredge, Colorado 81413 (mailing address)
TELEPHONE: 970-856-wine (9463)
WEBSITE: www.stoneymesa.com
TASTING ROOM HOURS: 11 A.M.–5 P.M. daily, closed winter holidays
WINE AVAILABILITY OUTSIDE WINERY: See website
PRICE RANGE OF WINES SOLD AT WINERY: $6.00–$15.00
WINE CLUB: No
ANNUAL PRODUCTION: 7,000 gallons
DIRECTIONS TO THE WINERY: Look for the signs on the south side of town on Highway 65. Turn west on 11th Avenue and follow it as it curves to a dead-end at 2125 Drive. Turn left and

watch for 2125 Drive as it goes up a hill to the right. Follow the road up the hill to the winery.

FACILITIES AND AMENITIES: Deck/gazebo, tasting room and gift shop, available for weddings, special events, and they have some summer concerts. Great view!

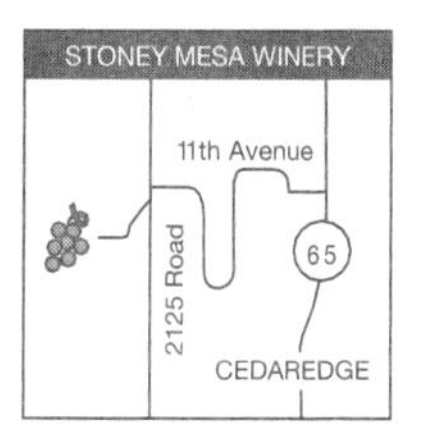

From father to son, the tradition of generations passing their businesses to the next; expansion, mixing the wisdom of the elder with the enthusiastic outlook of the younger would describe what is happening at Stoney Mesa Winery. Ron Neal has passed the winemaking duties to his son, Bret, and he has taken over as chief executive officer and public relations manager. Before going into the family business full time, Bret was the morning news director at KJCT television station in Grand Junction and also taught guitar. The extended family lives on the property, sharing the workload and, on a quiet summer evening, enjoying their view.

The first time we visited this hilltop winery, at 5,700 feet in elevation, Ron and his wife, Donna, and son lived in the 1880s farmhouse with a tiny building behind, which held the tasting room and another small building for their tanks and storage. Now, in only four years, there is a new house, the remodeled farmhouse/tasting room, a winery building and a gazebo fronted by 10 acres of vineyards.

With an ever-present eye on the future, they have invested in a wind machine to ward off any damaging freezes and have already broken ground for their new addition to be attached to the north side of the present building, which will house a climate-controlled barrel room that will hold 3,500 gallons and have 16-foot side walls for more barrel storage and a bottling room. This new addition will almost triple their size.

They also have a new distributor, Mountain Wine, owned by Gallo, who wants them to produce up to 5,000 cases in the next few years. "We'll be the only Colorado winery they'll carry in their portfolio. That will be an advantage," says Bret. At the distributor's suggestion, the Neals will concentrate on producing four wines: Merlot, Sauvignon Blanc, Riesling and Sunset Blush. They may add Gewürztraminer and Chardonnay.

Ron is still working on having a federal American Viticulture Area designation for the Surface Creek area near Cedaredge. Then he can say "Estate Bottled" on his labels. In fact, look for his new label, Ptarmigan Vineyards, which will be their select reserve and estate wines. They will continue to make wine under the Stoney Mesa label, keeping what the father began while paving the way for future generations.

WINE LIST

Cabernet Franc
Cabernet Sauvignon
Chardonnay
Gewürztraminer
Merlot
Riesling
Sauvignon
Sunset Blush

Surface Creek Winery

OWNERS' NAMES: Jim and Jeanne Durr
WINEMAKER: Jim Durr
YEAR LICENSED: 1999
ADDRESS: 2971 N Road, Eckert, Colorado 81418; P.O. Box 45, Eckert, Colorado 81418 (mailing address)
TELEPHONE: 970-835-wine (9463)
WEBSITE: www.surfacecreek.com
TASTING ROOM HOURS: In summer, 11 A.M.–5 P.M. daily. Please check their website or call them for winter hours.
WINE AVAILABILITY OUTSIDE WINERY: Currently available only at tasting room. Shipping in accordance with state and federal laws.

PRICE RANGE OF WINES SOLD AT WINERY: $7.50–$18.00
WINE CLUB: No
ANNUAL PRODUCTION: 2,000 gallons
DIRECTIONS TO THE WINERY: Eckert is located south of Cedaredge and northeast of Delta on Colorado Highway 65. Turn west at the stone church and Quest's High Country Wood Work. Go 0.5 mile and look for the white and stone house and large trees on your right.
FACILITIES AND AMENITIES: Gallery and tasting room

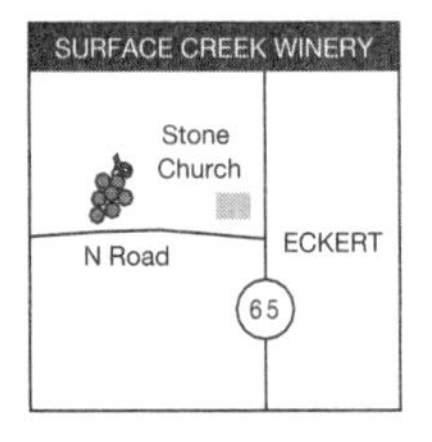

If you've never heard of Eckert, you're probably not alone. But with its proximity to the Grand Mesa and Palisade and the surprisingly balmy temperatures, it's well worth the trip. Jeanne and Jim Durr, who describe themselves as "recovering attorneys," were led to the area through their friendship with the Neal family at Stoney Mesa Winery. They would meet and talk about grapes and wine until the Durrs were so convinced about the merits of the area that they pulled up stakes in Fort Collins, bought some land at Eckert in the late 1990s and decided to grow grapes and enjoy country living.

At first, they planned only to grow and sell grapes. However, with Ron Neal's suggestions and help with their first crush, they took the plunge and decided to be a winery, which also involved a lot more work than originally planned. They've been learning more and more about winemaking ever since. They took advantage of advice from Richard Bruno, an oenologist and consultant hired by the Colorado Wine Industry Development Board. Bruno told them that good wine is easy to make, while good white wine is difficult to make. This has not deterred the Durrs. He gave specific suggestions that the Durrs say have enhanced their winemaking, especially since Chenin Blanc is their signature wine. "It's one of the future wines for Colorado," Jim says.

The first year they sold out of their Colorado Chenin Blanc, even after limiting customers to one bottle. Their 2001 release of Colorado Chenin Blanc is dry. For a distinctively different taste they will have a Chenin Blanc with grapes grown in Moab, Utah, which is their only non-Colorado wine. They have also chosen to make a slightly sweet cherry wine. Jim says the ability to grow cherries is a good indicator of whether or not you can grow high-end grape varieties. Bruno says their site might be a good one for Pinot Noir. Who knows what the future will bring?

In the immediate future, Surface Creek's production will reach 2,000–3,000 gallons. And they'll decide what to do then, but it might include buying a large orchard. They'll harvest their first Merlot and Chardonnay grapes in 2002, which will add to the other Colorado grapes they purchase from Delta, Montrose and Mesa Counties.

For the time being, you can enjoy a pleasant drive, turning west out of Eckert at the old stone church, coming soon to a white-fenced vineyard and stone-and-white farmhouse. Parking faces their gallery/tasting room with the red awning and lace-covered window. An indication of the charm within is the old wagon filled with flowers. The gallery features art from the Surface Creek Valley and other regional work. Enter the cool gallery to be greeted warmly by Jeanne and taste wine among the art—an agreeable combination!

WINE LIST

Blush Table Wine
Cabernet Sauvignon
Chenin Blanc
Cherry Wine
Colorado Chenin Blanc
Colorado Gewürztraminer
Colorado Merlot
White Table Wine

Sutcliffe
VINEYARDS

Cabernet Franc
Syrah
1999
McElmo Canyon, Colorado
Alcohol 12.1% By Volume

Sutcliffe Vineyards

OWNERS' NAMES: Emily and John Sutcliffe
WINEMAKER: John Sutcliffe
YEAR LICENSED: 1999
ADDRESS: 12202 Road G, Cortez, Colorado 81321-9510
TELEPHONE: 970-565-0825
WEBSITE: N/A
TASTING ROOM HOURS: Wednesdays 10 A.M.–4 P.M., but call ahead.

WINE AVAILABILITY OUTSIDE WINERY: Select restaurants and Cortez liquor stores. Will ship to legal states.
PRICE RANGE OF WINES SOLD AT WINERY: $10.00–$15.00
WINE CLUB: No
ANNUAL PRODUCTION: 500 gallons
DIRECTIONS TO THE WINERY: Take U.S. Highway 666 south of Cortez to McElmo Canyon Road (also named G Road or Airport Road), turning west at the M&M Truck Stop and driving about 14 miles. About 1 mile past a new bridge, look for a tall rock pinnacle (named Battle Rock) on the left with mail boxes on the right side of the road. Before reaching the rock, turn south down a dirt road, turning left again just past the first house on the left, about 100 yards. Keep following the dirt road and watch on the south for a yellow house with a nearby tower and a vineyard. That's the winery. Don't forget to call ahead.
FACILITIES AND AMENITIES: Tasting room. This is a working hay and livestock farm as well as a vineyard. Organic vegetables are for sale in season.

John Sutcliffe is one of those Renaissance men who seems to have done it all at one time or another. Making small quantities of premium wines is his latest effort. His winery, which he runs when he's not raising livestock or farming, is in one of the state's remotest spots, but his wine is found in some choice locations such as Telluride and New York City.

Sutcliffe was born into a noted British family (his father was on the board of Dunlop Ltd.) and he was an officer in the British Army. When his service ended, he moved to the United States, first to the Northeast but later to the West to become a cowboy. His first taste of Colorado came in 1968 when he went to work on a ranch in the Carbondale area.

His travels took him back to the southern United States, where he opened seven restaurants in Charleston, South Carolina, and Savannah, Georgia, giving him insights and friends in the restaurant industry. The contacts he has made have helped him spread the word about his wines.

Sutcliffe's wife, Emily, is an obstetrician/gynecologist who works in Cortez as well as donating her time at a Navajo hospital in Shiprock, New Mexico; a clinic in Monticello, Utah, and even in Mexico.

Sutcliffe bought the ranch in McElmo Canyon in 1990. He jokes that the previous owner had posted a sign on the road that said "Peaches, Melons and Ranch For Sale," and so he decided to "buy the whole bunch." The property came with some of the most senior water rights in the canyon, dating back to 1888, a valuable commodity in the desert. He has 200 acres total, of which 88 are irrigated.

Because he has always enjoyed good wine, Sutcliffe started planting his own grapes in 1995 (that first planting was frozen out, though, one of the hazards of the mile-high valley). He now has 10 acres of Merlot, Cabernet Franc, Syrah and Chardonnay vines, and he started making wine in small quantities in 1997.

"I never had time to study how to make wine so I sent my wines to restaurateurs to get their advice," he says. That's because he wants to sell primarily to restaurants and to produce wine that "very, very fussy people like."

Sutcliffe tosses out famous names of winery owners, restaurateurs and jet-setters who have visited his ranch and have helped him in one way or another. Among the spots carrying his wines is a resort in Telluride. One weekend a group from there, including Princess Caroline of Monaco, came for a visit. Because of his friendships, he has lined up three New York City restaurants to carry his wine. He also credits those in the Colorado wine industry for helping him with advice and selling him grapes.

Sutcliffe built his two-story adobe-like house, which lies across McElmo Creek near the foot of Sleeping Ute Mountain, one of the Ute Indian tribe's sacred mountains. His home is filled with books that display his wide range of tastes, including Turgenev, C.M. Russell, Matisse, Velasquez, Len Deighton, Tom Clancy, Umberto Eco and James Joyce. Crimson-red geraniums nearly 5 feet tall crowded the west windows in his living room the day we visited.

WINE LIST

Cabernet Franc/Syrah
Chardonnay
Chenin Blanc (under a McElmo Canyon Wines label)
Merlot

Terror Creek Winery

OWNERS' NAMES: John and Joan Mathewson
WINEMAKER: Joan Mathewson
YEAR LICENSED: 1992
ADDRESS: 1750 4175 Drive, Paonia, Colorado 81428
TELEPHONE: 970-527-3484
WEBSITE: N/A
TASTING ROOM HOURS: 11 A.M.–5 P.M. Friday, Saturday and Sunday from Memorial Day through Labor Day
WINE AVAILABILITY OUTSIDE WINERY: In select liquor stores and restaurants in Denver metro area, Boulder, Grand Junction, Carbondale, Redstone, Paonia and Hotchkiss
PRICE RANGE OF WINES SOLD AT WINERY: $10.50–$16.00
WINE CLUB: No
ANNUAL PRODUCTION: 2,000 gallons

DIRECTIONS TO THE WINERY: Drive to Paonia on Colorado Highway 133. From the east, the most direct route is from Glenwood Springs past Carbondale over McClure Pass. From the west the best route is from Delta through Hotchkiss, although the most scenic route is over the Grand Mesa through Cedaredge. The winery and vineyards are on the mesa north of Paonia. Colorado Highway 133 doesn't go through Paonia, so start from the stop sign on the highway where the business loop connects with the highway. Drive east about a half-mile and watch for a dirt road heading north up to the mesa (the road is 4175 Drive, marked with a small street sign and Terror Creek has a sign there as well). The road is just west of the Bowie Mine #1 and its three silos on the south side of the highway. Drive up 4175 Road heading generally north about two miles. You can see the winery across about 10 acres of vineyards where the road ends.

FACILITIES AND AMENITIES: There is a tasting room, but no gift shop or food. Public restrooms are available. A picnic area is on the lawn outside.

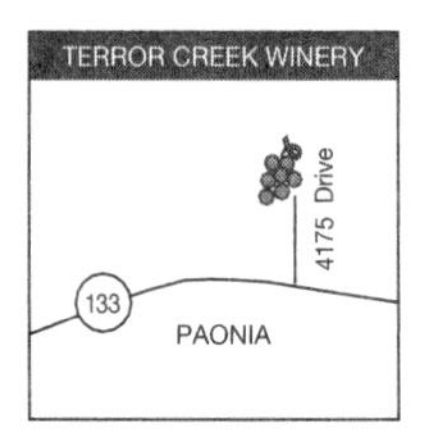

For the best view from a Colorado winery—and perhaps any winery in the world—take your car up Garvin Mesa north of the Western Slope town of Paonia. At the end of the road is 6,400-foot Terror Creek Winery, named for the stream that washes the mesa. From the small parking lot look across the North Fork of Gunnison River Valley to Landsend and Lamborn Peaks and on to the West Elk Mountains.

If this reminds you of Switzerland, it is appropriate. That's where Joan Mathewson learned her winemaking skills—she's the only winemaker in the state with a degree from a Swiss wine college—and that's one of the reasons the Mathewsons chose the winery's location when John retired from the oil business in 1990.

As you would expect, Joan makes her wines in a style typical of Swiss wines, especially of the Alsace region of northern France. She makes a dry Gewürztraminer and Riesling (unlike the sweet wines made from these grapes in Germany), an unoaked Chardonnay and a fruity Pinot Noir. In 1999, she started making a red table wine that is a blend of Pinot Noir and Gamay, similar to a Swiss Gamay Dole and may try her hand at some other Swiss-style blends.

Because the Swiss wine industry is so small and little of their production is exported, this may be the best place in the United

States to taste a Swiss-style wine. Joan learned her craft when she took summer trips to Switzerland while John was working in the oil business in the Middle East. In order to attend the Swiss wine college (you can see her diploma on the wall behind the tasting room bar), Joan had to learn French. She says she still thinks in French when she's making wine.

The Mathewsons have 10 acres of vines, not including some experimental vines that Colorado State University planted in the 1970s on their property to see how they would do at 6,400-feet elevation. That altitude makes Terror Creek the highest winery in the country and perhaps the world.

When you arrive at the winery you may be greeted by Maggie, Joan's border collie, although she often lies in the shade during the summer. The Mathewsons have tables and lawn chairs set up under the shade trees for guests to sip wine and marvel at the view.

Both Mathewsons went to college in Colorado, John at the Colorado School of Mines and Joan at the former Colorado Women's College, but they spent their working lives elsewhere as John traveled the oil-and-gas circuit in the United States and other countries. They kept returning to Colorado on vacation and decided to locate their winery in the state when John retired. Of course, they have discovered that retiring to run a winery has not lessened the workload.

WINE LIST

Chardonnay
Dry Riesling
Gewürztraminer
Pinot Noir
Red Table Wine

WITHOUT TASTING ROOMS

Puesta del Sol Winery

OWNERS' NAMES: Eames and Pam Petersen
WINEMAKER: Eames Petersen
YEAR LICENSED: 2000
ADDRESS: 1189 4050 Road, Paonia, Colorado 81428
TELEPHONE: 970-527-6296
WEBSITE: N/A
TASTINGS: None at present
WINE AVAILABILITY OUTSIDE WINERY: Sold in stores and restaurants on the Western Slope.
PRICE RANGE OF WINES SOLD AT WINERY: $10.00–$15.00
WINE CLUB: No

ANNUAL PRODUCTION: 1,000 gallons

DIRECTIONS TO THE WINERY: Located south of Paonia, but not currently open to the public. May open a tasting room in the future.

FACILITIES AND AMENITIES: None

Eames and Pam Petersen, owners of the Puesta del Sol Winery near Paonia, have some grape-growing methods you might not find in the textbooks. Pam planted roses at the end of each row of vines after hearing that they would draw away disease that might affect the grapes. They also play music, usually classical, to the grapes as they ripen. Both of the Petersens are musicians, Eames a classical guitarist and Pam on the keyboard and piano. They started playing music to the grapes in 1995 when they planted their first grapes on 3 acres of land. Two years later they didn't play to the grapes, and a freeze damaged the vines. Now they're afraid not to play to the vines. Pam even wrote a song, informally named "The Grape Song," which she says came to her while she was working in the vineyard. "The grapes spoke to me," she says.

"Puesta del Sol" gets its name from the Spanish term for "sunset," and from the backyard of the Petersen's 1950s log house the sunsets are spectacular, looking west as the land rolls away toward the North Fork of the Gunnison River.

Petersen has been making small quantities of wine for several years, received his limited winery license in 2000 and built a winery in 2001. His first wines, both a 2000 vintage totaling about 300 cases, are a Pinot Noir and a red table wine blended from Cabernet Franc, Cabernet Sauvignon and Merlot grapes.

Steve Rhodes, the owner of nearby S. Rhodes Winery, was Petersen's wine mentor, encouraging him to use an open vat fermentation process and to "let the grapes speak for themselves" by not adding anything during the wine-making process.

Puesta del Sol's winery building was designed to have a tasting room and Petersen may sell wine at the winery in the future. For now, however, he wants to see how well his wine is received in Western Slope restaurants and liquor stores. And, perhaps, to see what composer the grapes like the best.

WINE LIST

Pinot Noir
Red Table Wine

S. Rhodes Vineyards

OWNER'S NAME: Steve Rhodes
WINEMAKER: Steve Rhodes
YEAR LICENSED: 1996
ADDRESS: Hotchkiss, Colorado 81419
TELEPHONE: 970-527-5185
WEBSITE: N/A
TASTINGS: By appointment only
WINE AVAILABILITY OUTSIDE WINERY: Primarily sold in restaurants and liquor stores in Aspen, Vail, Telluride and a few in the Denver area.
PRICE RANGE OF WINES SOLD AT WINERY: N/A (usually sold by the case)
WINE CLUB: N/A (but sells by invitation to buyers list)
ANNUAL PRODUCTION: 2,400 gallons

DIRECTIONS TO THE WINERY: N/A
FACILITIES AND AMENITIES AT THE WINERY: None

First of all, Steve Rhodes didn't even want to be in this book. That tells you a lot about his business philosophy, which may qualify him as one of those "crazy like a fox" entrepreneurs. Rhodes makes small quantities of wine at his parent's former farm near Hotchkiss. He has built a reputation locally and in restaurants and stores in Colorado's resorts. But he insists he doesn't want to get any bigger and he especially doesn't want any tourists driving their Winnebagoes down the dirt road to his winery. That's why he swore us to secrecy about his winery's location.

"I only want to sell to real wine people," he says. "If I haven't met them or have a recommendation from someone; I don't want them coming here." This may make Rhodes sound exclusive and reclusive, which is only partially true.

When we first tracked him down at his winery on a hot September afternoon, he couldn't have been more friendly. He and a friend had just completed crushing a batch of grapes. Rhodes stopped what he was doing, showed us the open vats he uses for fermentation, the storage tanks and the cool wine cellar for barrel aging. He offered us tastes directly from the barrel, which is the only way you can taste his wine unless you buy it.

Rhodes's wines can be purchased by the bottle only in some liquor stores. You can buy it by the glass in restaurants like The Little Nell in Aspen, Krabloonik near Snowmass and the Woody Creek Tavern (where his reds are the house wine) outside Aspen. Or you can buy it by the case at his winery if you are on Rhodes's list or are referred by one of his clients.

That does make S. Rhodes wines exclusive—and exclusivity can pay off—but part of the reason he limits his sales is that he doesn't want to get any bigger. "I don't believe things have to grow to be good," he says. "You can sustain a business without growing. Sometimes you can do quite well with a little home business and then lose it if you expand. I don't believe in endless growth."

Rhodes has 7.5 acres of grapes—Merlot, Pinot Noir and Gewürztraminer—and buys Chardonnay and Cabernet Franc from other growers. Usually these are Colorado grapes, but sometimes he gets them from California if he can't find what he wants in the state. He makes wines from the grapes he has available, so you won't find all the varieties every year.

He started out by selling his wines for around $10–$12 a bottle, but he raised his prices (we paid $17 a bottle in Denver in 2001) because his costs—mostly shipping—kept climbing. That price is getting a little steep for the average consumer. But Rhodes isn't after the average customer.

WINE LIST (depending on availability)

Cabernet Franc
Cabernet Sauvignon
Chardonnay
Gewürztraminer
Merlot
Pinot Noir
Table Red

WATCH FOR

Bienvenu Vineyards

By the middle of this decade, there may be a new winery in the Hotchkiss area using a French hybrid grape that most people are unfamiliar with. Yvon Gros, who runs the Leroux Creek Inn (see listing under accommodations) and Bienvenu Vineyards, planted a small plot of Chambourcin grapes in 1998 outside his inn and had his first harvest in 2001. If Mother Nature is kind and financing is available, he will plant additional vines that will be mature by about 2004, and Gros will open his winery.

Chambourcin is a French hybrid developed in the middle of the twentieth century, which Gros, who is a native Frenchman, says apparently was made from Merlot and Cabernet Sauvignon stock. He has five acres available to plant in vines and has been making wine from purchased grapes in limited quantities.

Jim Durr at Surface Creek Winery has been Gros's mentor for winemaking. Gros has had long experience with wine, however, having been in the hotel and restaurant business in Vail for 25 years before moving to the North Fork of the Gunnison Valley. If you stay at Gros's inn, ask to stay for dinner, which he cooks using local produce and meats.

ACCOMMODATIONS AND DINING

ACCOMMODATIONS

BRAHAM'S INN

1258 Highway 65
Eckert, Colorado 81418 (Surface Creek Valley area)
970-835-3357
Hosts: Frank and Judy Braham
This remodeled fruit-packing shed built in 1920 has five large rooms with a deck and serves a full breakfast—or very full some would say.

BROSS HOTEL

312 Onega St.; P.O. Box 85
Paonia, Colorado 81428 (near Terror Creek Winery and Puesta del Sol Winery)
970-527-6776
Hostesses: Linda Lentz and her daughter, Susan Steinhardt
This 1906 renovated hotel has ten rooms and serves full breakfasts in the dining room. You'll have fun looking at the murals of people near the elevator on each floor. Take a relaxing stroll around this little town.

LEROUX CREEK INN AND BIENVENU VINEYARDS

1200 3100 Road; P.O. Box 910
Hotchkiss, Colorado 81419
970-872-4746
Hosts: Yvon Gros and Joanna Gilbert
The southwestern-styled adobe B&B sits on 46 acres with five big rooms, a living room with fireplace, a deck where breakfast is often served, an outdoor hot tub, and hearty breakfasts made by Yvon, a trained chef. He will also do dinners if given notice. There is a peace here as you gaze across the landscape. (See related write-up on Bienvenu Vineyards on page 91.)

DINING

BERARDI'S RESTAURANT AT DEER CREEK (PUBLIC GOLF COURSE)

500 S.E. Jay Avenue
Cedaredge, Colorado 81413
970-856-7781

The chef here came highly recommended and, as Brad said, it was a surprise to find food like this in a golf course restaurant. Good pasta dishes representing differing regions of Italy. Open daily 11 A.M.–4 P.M. for lunch, 5 P.M.–9 P.M. for dinner. Reservations accepted.

MAD DOG RANCH

131 Highway 92; P.O. Box 424
Crawford, Colorado 81415
970-921-SODA
Website: www.cocker.com/mdrfc

This is a side trip that takes you to Crawford, some good food, a great outdoor patio and the chance to say you ate at Joe Cocker's place. For those of you not-in-the-know, he's a country/rock singer. The nicest part of this is seeing and learning about how many good changes the Cockers have made in their community.

RUSSELL STOVER FACTORY OUTLET STORE

2185 Stover Avenue
Montrose, Colorado 81401
970-249-5372

Okay, so it's not a restaurant, but there are samples everywhere and nobody's checking how many you have. Well, maybe it is a wine-related destination; think how good chocolate is as an after dinner treat with some fine Colorado dessert wines.

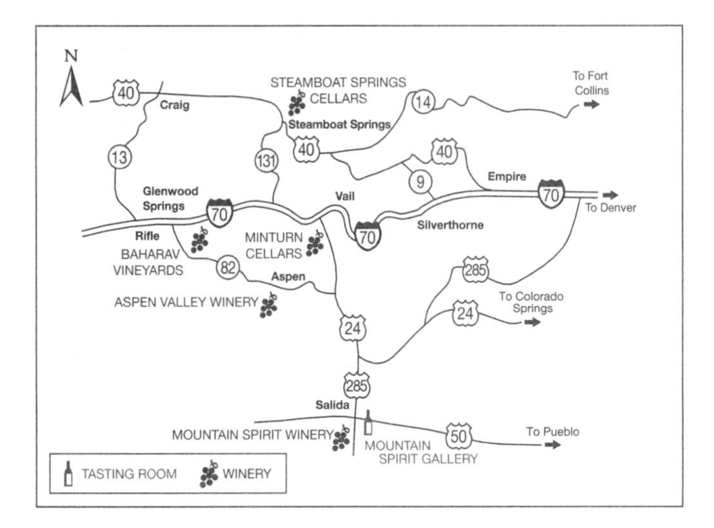
N
STEAMBOAT SPRINGS CELLARS
To Fort Collins
40
Craig
14
Steamboat Springs
40
13
131
40
9
Empire
Glenwood Springs
Vail
70
70
To Denver
70
Silverthorne
Rifle
MINTURN CELLARS
BAHARAV VINEYARDS
82
Aspen
285
ASPEN VALLEY WINERY
To Colorado Springs
24
24
285
Salida
MOUNTAIN SPIRIT WINERY
50
To Pueblo
MOUNTAIN SPIRIT GALLERY
TASTING ROOM
WINERY

MOUNTAIN WINERIES

Baharav Vineyards

OWNERS' NAMES: Eva and Dan Baharav
WINEMAKER: Dan Baharav
YEAR LICENSED: 1999
ADDRESS: 2370 Road 112, Carbondale, Colorado 81623
TELEPHONE: 970-963-9659 or 877-ECO-WINE (877-326-9463)
WEBSITE: N/A (e-mail: baharavs@sopris.net)
TASTING ROOM HOURS: By invitation only
WINE AVAILABILITY OUTSIDE WINERY: Some restaurants
PRICE RANGE OF WINES SOLD AT WINERY: $16.00–$20.00

WINE CLUB: No

ANNUAL PRODUCTION: 2,000 gallons

DIRECTIONS TO THE WINERY: From Glenwood Springs take Colorado Highway 82 south toward Carbondale. About 8 miles south of Glenwood watch for the Go Kart raceway on the east side of the road and turn left onto a frontage road (the turn is a half-mile past the Sopris Restaurant on the highway). Take County Road 113, also called Cattle Creek Road, for 3.7 miles as it climbs into the hills. Turn right onto County Road 112 and follow it up a canyon about 1 mile. Turn left at the first driveway and the house is nestled in the pines. There is a sign. Call ahead to make sure someone is there.

FACILITIES AND AMENITIES: Tasting room

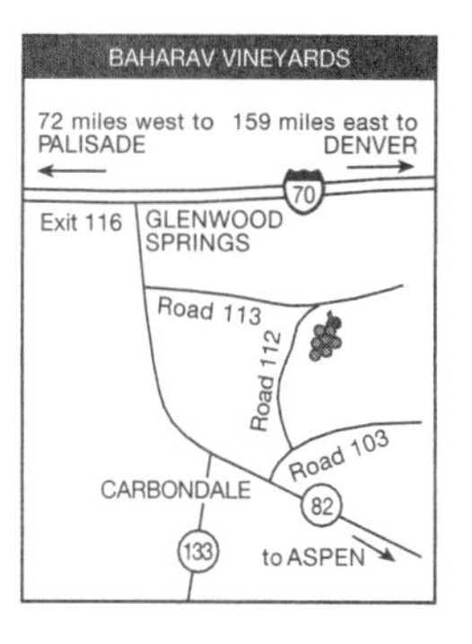

Dan Baharav has a doctorate in ecology and is an environmental consultant. That fact alone provides an insight into what kind of wines he is making. Everything he does is done as close to nature's intentions as possible.

A native of Israel, Baharav makes small quantities of wines in the garage of his home on a back road in the hills above Carbondale. But he gets his grapes from his own 15-acre vineyard on East Orchard Mesa near Palisade. He bought the property, already planted with 5 acres of Chardonnay, in 1993 and since has planted Cabernet Franc, Merlot, Syrah, Viognier and Muscat grapes.

The grapes he farms, Baharav says, are as close to being organically grown as possible. He uses only natural fertilizers, adds no chemicals to the wine and uses no chemicals in the vineyard except sulfur dust to control powdery mildew. He lets the natural vegetation grow between the vines. He limits the use of a tractor because he doesn't want to damage the soil. Few other Colorado wineries follow the same practices. Baharav only uses his own grapes in his wine, but he does sell grapes to other winemakers.

The winery has another distinction—almost all of its wines are sold at by-invitation parties to people who live in the Roaring Fork Valley, by appointment or by shipment. You can't buy it in liquor stores.

That may change in the future—they have acquired a spot and a license to open a tasting room along Colorado Highway 82 between Carbondale and Glenwood Springs—but for now they usually sell out of their limited quantities in five or six weeks.

"I don't want my wine sitting around in a warehouse for a year, going bad and then people blaming me," he says. "I want to keep things small and I can control it."

WINE LIST

Cabernet Franc/Merlot blend
Chardonnay
Merlot
Viognier

Minturn Cellars

OWNERS' NAMES: Taffy and Bruce McLaughlin
WINEMAKER: Bruce McLaughlin
YEAR LICENSED: 1990
ADDRESS: 107 Williams Street, Minturn, Colorado 81645
TELEPHONE: 970-827-4065
WEBSITE: N/A
TASTING ROOM HOURS: In summer, 10 A.M.–5 P.M. Wednesday–Saturday, and 12 P.M.–3 P.M. Sunday–Tuesday. In winter, 12 P.M.–5 P.M. weekends.
WINE AVAILABILITY OUTSIDE WINERY: At the Wines of Colorado store on U.S. Highway 24 near Cascade, at the turnoff to the Pikes Peak Highway. The store is an off-site tasting room run by the McLaughlins, featuring wines from many Colorado wineries.
PRICE RANGE OF WINES SOLD AT WINERY: All wines $15.00 per bottle

WINE CLUB: No
ANNUAL PRODUCTION: 2,000 gallons
DIRECTIONS TO THE WINERY: From I-70, take Exit 171, go south on U.S. Highway 24 for 2 miles. As you enter Minturn, a restaurant, Chili Willy's, is on your right with the Minturn Country Club west of it. The winery is in an alley directly behind the two restaurants.
FACILITIES AND AMENITIES: Space upstairs for private parties. There are some gift baskets and other items for sale in the tasting room.

As Vail has spread its "haute" lifestyle down-valley toward Avon and Eagle, funky little Minturn has not escaped its influence. But the town built as a railroad roundabout station continues to keep some of its old unique charms. Part of that is Minturn Cellars, nestled into a hillside in an alley behind two town institutions, Chilly Willy's and Minturn Country Club.

Minturn Cellars was converted from a two-bedroom house that had a garage on the alley behind the two restaurants. Owner and winemaker, Bruce McLaughlin, converted the garage into a winery, and his wife, Taffy, used part of the garage for a tasting room.

McLaughlin, who started his own winery in 1976 in Newtown, Connecticut, was drawn to the Vail area by his older brother, who moved to the resort in 1962. His first stop in Colorado, however, was in Colorado Springs, where he became part owner and winemaker at one of the state's oldest wineries, Pikes Peak Vineyards. He still trades his time between the two.

McLaughlin's brother had purchased the old house in Minturn, and Bruce converted it into a wine-making operation, figuring that "skiers don't make it to Palisade, but they'll come to Minturn."

Instinctive when it comes to making wine, McLaughlin buys grapes from numerous vineyards around the state. Some of his offerings change from year to year, depending on the availability of grape varieties, but it normally has the standard varietals. One year he made a white Muscat. More recently he added a Port-style dessert wine.

WINE LIST

Cabernet Sauvignon
Chardonnay
Merlot
Port
Shiraz (Syrah)
Viognier

Mountain Spirit Winery, Ltd.

OWNERS' NAMES: Terry and Michael Barkett
WINEMAKERS: Terry and Michael Barkett
YEAR LICENSED: 1995
ADDRESS: Winery is at 15750 County Road 220, Salida, Colorado 81201; Gallery and tasting room at 201 F Street, Salida, Colorado 81201
TELEPHONE: Winery (719-539-1175); Gallery (719-539-7848)
WEBSITE: www.mountainspiritwinery.com
TASTING ROOM HOURS: Gallery—10 A.M.–5 P.M. Monday–Saturday. Winery—11 A.M.–5:00 P.M., Monday, Thursday, Friday and Saturday.

WINE AVAILABILITY OUTSIDE WINERY: Only at winery and gallery/tasting room and the store Wines of Colorado in Cascade, Colorado.

PRICE RANGE OF WINES SOLD AT WINERY: $9.50–$14.95

WINE CLUB: Yes

ANNUAL PRODUCTION: 5,000 gallons

DIRECTIONS TO THE WINERY: Winery is located 13 miles west of Salida and 5 miles west of Poncha Springs off U.S. Highway 50, turn onto County Road 220. Watch for sign on U.S. Highway 50 or visit tasting room/gallery in downtown Salida, Colorado.

FACILITIES AND AMENITIES: Tasting room inside gallery and winery has a beautiful setting for events.

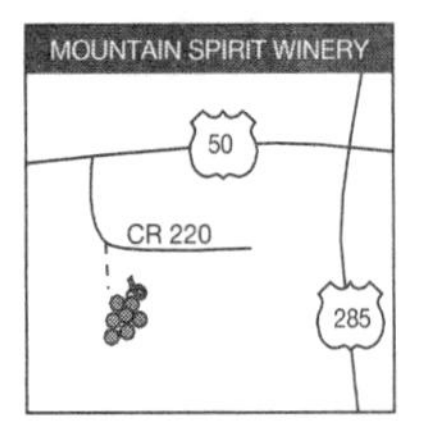

Michael and Terry Barkett wanted to have a state-of-the-art equipped winery. To that end, they researched other wineries in Colorado before designing their own. Michael, a physician in Salida, is particularly proud of his sparkling wine lab.

The Barketts offer wines with some residual sugar and unique grape/fruit blends, which they say are offered nowhere else in the world. They are unable to grow grapes at their 8,000-foot altitude but have their own chokecherries and raspberries for dessert wines and blends.

They blend raspberries with Merlot. Terry calls another blend, their Blackberry/Cabernet Franc, the "relationship-saver" because grape wine lovers and fruit wine lovers both enjoy it. Humans aren't the only ones who love their fruit. In the fall of 2001 they built a $12,000 fence around the chokecherries, but a bear still broke through the gate to get them. The Barketts tell their customers that their distinctively different wines can be paired with almost any food. They want wine drinking to become an everyday experience, not just for special occasions.

Their winery is in a pastoral setting along a stream on the east side of Monarch Pass. The historic 5-acre homestead with 80-year-old apple trees is particularly pleasant on a summer evening. Musical performances are scheduled in the summer on the expanded loading dock of the winery building. They have put in new professional lighting, and on performance evenings there is a cheese tasting or buffet, plus wine, of course, by the glass. Seating is outside and the limited tickets need to be purchased early. If the weather is inclement, the performances are held inside the winery.

If you're in Salida, you'll want to stop downtown at their gallery/tasting room, a former bank on a downtown corner, which displays Terry's artwork as well as many local artists. In the "wine vault" are wine accessories and gift baskets with Mountain Spirit wine. This "artsy" connection can be seen on their wine labels. The Mountain Spirit Winery label designed by a Salida artist, Pat Oglesley, is a Southwestern-styled angel that reminds one of the "snow angel" on nearby Mount Shavano. Their new dessert wine label was designed by another local artist, Gloria Jean Countryman; some of her landscapes can be seen in the gallery.

If you enjoy art, watch for dates of artists' receptions and street entertainment on Friday nights during the summer and Salida's "Art Walk" the last weekend in June.

WINE LIST

Angel Blush
Blackberry/Cabernet Franc
Blackberry/Chardonnay
Chardonnay
Merlot
Merlot/Raspberry
Riesling/Chardonnay

Dessert Wines

Chokecherry
Raspberry

WITHOUT TASTING ROOMS OR OPENING SOON

Aspen Valley Winery

OWNERS' NAMES: Patrick Leto, Katie Leto, John Francis
WINEMAKER: Patrick Leto
YEAR LICENSED: 1997
ADDRESS: 197 Coyote Circle, Carbondale, Colorado 81623
TELEPHONE: 970-704-WINE (9463)
WEBSITE: www.aspenwine.com

TASTING ROOM HOURS: N/A
WINE AVAILABILITY OUTSIDE WINERY: Purchase off the website or at the Aspen Farmer's Market on East Hopkins Avenue in Aspen, open Saturdays 8 A.M.–4 P.M., June 1 through October 31.
PRICE RANGE OF WINES: $12.00–$25.00
WINE CLUB: No
ANNUAL PRODUCTION IN GALLONS: N/A
DIRECTIONS TO THE WINERY: N/A
FACILITIES AND AMENITIES: N/A

When Patrick Leto's wife, Katie, gave him a Father's Day present in 1991 he didn't know it would change his life. Receiving the gift, he says, "was a dream come true. It was the best Father's Day of my whole life."

The gift was a trip to Palisade to visit Colorado's four existing wineries. One of those he visited was Grande River Vineyards, which Stephen Smith had opened a year earlier. He met Smith, got into an excited conversation with him about making wine and "a half-hour later we were crawling over barrels, tasting wine and talking."

Leto, who is of Italian heritage, had another influence to get him into the winery business. He says there is an Italian legend that if a man reaches the age of forty without making his own wine something bad will happen to him. That day was closing in on him in 1991 so he asked Smith to help him.

Leto, who lives in the Carbondale area and manages the mall at Snowmass Village, bought grapes from Smith's vineyard and made wine for a couple of years just to learn the process.

"The first Merlot I made was exactly the way he (Smith) said to do it," he says. "During that process I probably put in a dozen calls to him with questions. Before I made it, we did a taste of several Merlots and I told him which one I liked. He said he'd show me how."

In 1996, Leto sent a bottle of his 1994 Merlot to the Colorado State Fair, where it won an award as the best amateur red wine. The label was drawn by Leto's daughter, Alicia, who was seven at the time.

From that point on things began to snowball for Leto and two friends, Tony Brevetti and John Francis, who helped him start the winery in 1997. The *Snowmass Sun* wrote a story about Leto's wine, and the story was picked up by the Associated Press and published in newspapers around the country. The Aspen name, of course, has a certain cachet and when you put it together with a product like wine it generates attention.

Out of the ordinary, even for Aspen, was that they were making the wine in Brevetti's gasoline station in Carbondale. Brevetti left the partnership in 2000 to open his own winery, Snowmass Creek Winery (see separate write-up on page 110), and Leto started making wine at his home.

Much of Leto's small production of three red wine styles is sold at the Aspen Farmer's Market. He also sells white wines from other Colorado wineries there, including Grande River, Carlson Vineyards, Cottonwood Cellars and Rocky Mountain Meadery. He also sells over the Internet and through some Aspen area restaurants.

Leto won't disclose how much his annual production is, but his capacity is about 1,500 gallons. He buys his grapes from Palisade vineyards, including Grande River and Baharav Vineyards. Sometime in the future Leto wants to open a tasting room in the Palisade area, but probably not until his children, Alicia and Ryan, are grown.

Leto is unabashed when he says that his wines "are a great tourist product. I sell a lot to people who are looking for gifts to take home from Aspen, just like T-shirts. Aspen is a fantastic market."

WINE LIST

Cabernet Franc
Merlot
Red Table

Steamboat Springs Cellars

OWNERS' NAMES: Tom and Kathie Williams
WINEMAKER: Tom Williams
YEAR LICENSED: 1998
ADDRESS: 2900 West Acres Drive #89, Steamboat Springs, Colorado 80487
TELEPHONE: 970-879-7501
WEBSITE: N/A (e-mail: stickyf@cmn.net)
TASTING ROOM HOURS: By appointment only
WINE AVAILABILITY OUTSIDE WINERY: Liquor stores in Steamboat Springs; major liquor stores in Denver and Grand Junction.
PRICE RANGE OF WINES SOLD AT WINERY: $13.50–$16.50
WINE CLUB: No
ANNUAL PRODUCTION: 1,800 gallons
DIRECTIONS TO THE WINERY: West on Highway 40 from Steamboat Springs. Turn right at NAPA Auto Parts store onto Downhill Drive. Turn right at 2464 Downhill Drive to Unit 8.
FACILITIES AND AMENITIES: Tastings

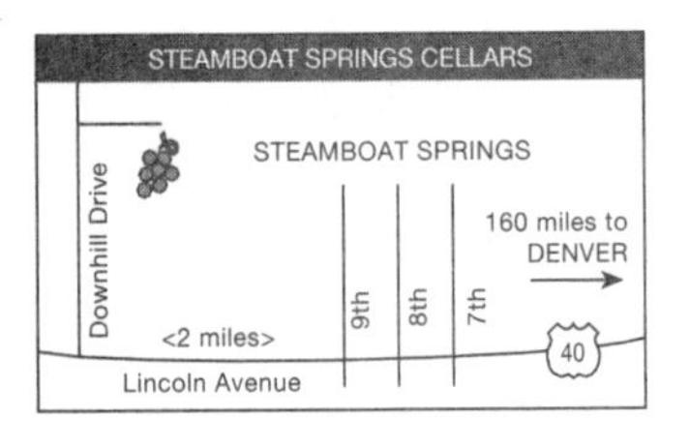

In 1997, we were selling our books at a wine festival when a nice couple came up to chat. They said they were going to start a winery in Steamboat Springs and could they contact us when they opened. To be honest, we had heard this kind of thing before, usually from people who had no idea about all the problems involved with this business. However, these two were serious and in early 1999 we received a note and a business card from Tom and Kathie Williams saying they had opened Steamboat Springs Cellars.

Of course, they don't grow fruit there. They buy Colorado grapes; some from Stephen Smith at Grande River Vineyards, and they have been buying California strawberries through their local City Market grocery store, 1,000 pounds at a time.

Asked how they began, Tom says, "I ordered a can of grape juice concentrate and made wine in the kitchen. After four years of making it for family and friends, I decided to try it (commercial winemaking). I wanted to do it because I enjoy it; I want to make quality wine."

That was 1993. He and Kathie went to the premier wine school in the country, the University of California–Davis, four or five times to take weekend wine classes. Additionally, there they met oenologist Joe Davis and hired him as their wine consultant. "We used him a lot at first, but it's limited now because I've learned a lot," Tom notes. Tom's wine is unfiltered he says, because, "I like to do as little as possible to the wine." He uses French oak for his whites and American oak for his reds. When asked how long he barrel-aged, he charmingly replies, "Until I need the barrel." Seriously, he likes to age them for 12-to-16 months or longer.

Notice his labels; he's really kept the local flavor. Each of the blends denotes a regional site familiar to most such as Rabbit Ears Red (the pass coming into town), Strawberry Park (a legendary hot springs east of Steamboat Springs) and Fish Creek Falls (a good hiking destination and used by Coors on their original label). Also, their label, by local artist Elizabeth Whitmore, is a rendition of the oft-photographed old barn at the foot of Steamboat Ski Resort.

If you want to pick up a souvenir, besides a bottle of wine, Tom sells bottle-balancers by putting a hole in a short length of an old barrel stave (the wooden staves used to make barrels) to hold the bottle at a 90-degree angle in the air in perfect balance. Take a drive and visit this picturesque area. On Saturday afternoons in the summer, you'll find Tom in downtown Steamboat Springs across from the courthouse in his remote tasting room "tent."

WINE LIST

Chardonnay
Fish Creek Falls (Sauvignon Blanc)
Merlot
Rabbit Ears Red
Strawberry Park (Riesling blend)

WATCH FOR

Snowmass Creek Winery

Another mountain winery that plans to open in the summer of 2002 is the Snowmass Creek Winery in the Aspen area. Tony Brevetti and Bill Welcher are co-owners and the winemakers. Tony first partnered with Patrick Leto and John Francis at Aspen Valley Winery and later their partnership ended, but it didn't quell Tony's desire to make wine.

Brevetti and Welcher bought a 7-acre vineyard on East Orchard Mesa near Palisade where vines had been planted fifteen years earlier. They will have wines from all Colorado grapes, including the varietals Merlot, Cabernet Franc, Chardonnay and Riesling. Look for their opening on Old Snowmass Highway 82, but call first (970-927-3633). Their tasting room will be by appointment only.

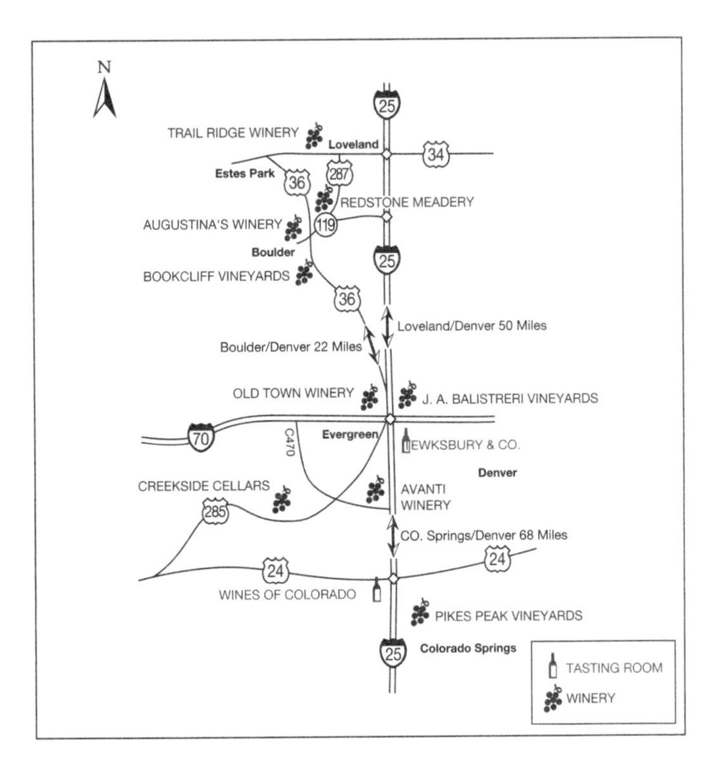

N
25
TRAIL RIDGE WINERY
Loveland
34
Estes Park
36
287
REDSTONE MEADERY
AUGUSTINA'S WINERY
119
Boulder
25
BOOKCLIFF VINEYARDS
36
Loveland/Denver 50 Miles
Boulder/Denver 22 Miles
OLD TOWN WINERY
J. A. BALISTRERI VINEYARDS
70
C470
Evergreen
TEWKSBURY & CO.
Denver
CREEKSIDE CELLARS
AVANTI
WINERY
285
CO. Springs/Denver 68 Miles
24
24
WINES OF COLORADO
PIKES PEAK VINEYARDS
25
Colorado Springs
TASTING ROOM
WINERY

FRONT RANGE WINERIES

Augustina's Winery

OWNER'S NAME: Marianne "Gussie" Walter
WINEMAKER: Marianne Walter
YEAR LICENSED: 1997
ADDRESS: 4715 N. Broadway B-3, Boulder, Colorado 80304
TELEPHONE: 303-545-2047
WEBSITE: N/A
TASTING ROOM HOURS: Varies seasonally—call for current hours
WINE AVAILABILITY OUTSIDE WINERY: Boulder liquor stores and the Boulder County Farmers' Market, and Colorado mountain markets in Evergreen and Winter Park. Will ship.

PRICE RANGE OF WINES SOLD AT WINERY: $7.00–$12.00
WINE CLUB: No
ANNUAL PRODUCTION: 1,100 gallons
DIRECTIONS TO THE WINERY: Drive north on Broadway, turn west a half-block north of Broadway and Yarmouth Avenue at the greenhouse/nursery. The winery is on the south side of the building behind the greenhouse.
FACILITIES AND AMENITIES: Tastings at the winery

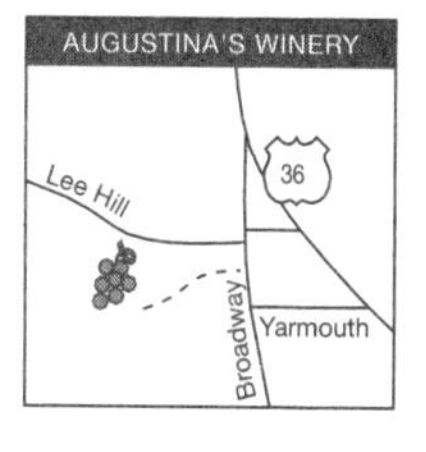

A winery was not even a glimmer for Marianne Walter when she came to Boulder in 1982 for graduate school at the University of Colorado. She's a geologist by profession and worked for the U.S. Geological Service until 1995. She decided to "drop out," and, having been a home winemaker for a while, chose to be an apprentice at Black Mesa Winery in New Mexico. After a year and a half, she returned to Colorado, knowing she wanted to make wine. In early 1997 she got her license for Augustina's Winery and made her first wine that fall. She has picked up all kinds of jobs, including working in Loveland for Trail Ridge Winery and at a wine shop. Marianne says the winery pays for itself but not her living expenses. She started up originally in Erie, but had to find another space. She now has her tasting room/winery in a warehouse space that she says, "is a workable situation, not the most attractive." In the future she would like to have her home and winery in the same place, but it would have to be out of Boulder's city limits (to be affordable).

Asked about the winery name, she says, "As a child, I was tagged with the nickname 'Gussie.'" She never liked it, but now accepts it and instead of using a geographic name, chose Augustina's because it could have been the root for her nickname.

Her labels and wine reflect her lively, active personality and her *joie de vivre*. In fact, she uses "Joie de Vino" as the varietal label for her Chardonnay. Her philosophy is on the back label: "Dedicated to making wines that go with backpacking adventures, raucous poker parties, family barbecues, good mystery novels, and gingersnaps." Her distinctive diamond-shaped labels were her ideas, translated by a graphic designer. Her "WineChick" logo with a stylized 1940s pin-up girl is so much "fun" that someone once stole her winery sign (as a college prank?).

"Sometimes wine can be a little uptight, so I have fun with the labels," Marianne says. However, make no mistake, this is a competent winemaker. She says she writes everything down, trying to be consistent in her winemaking. "Notes. It's a geologist thing," she says.

Marianne has received compliments from fellow winemakers. She bought her Lemberger grapes for her WineChick Red from Parker Carlson (Carlson Vineyards) who said that "her Lemberger from our grapes is outstanding." That's a mouthful since Parker also uses his Lemberger in his own well-received Tyrannosaurus Red.

When asked if she had a signature wine, Marianne says, "No, but a signature style of distinct tastes. I want to make sure they're interesting." Some of the distinctiveness may come from the fact that she plays blues music to her wine as it ages.

The future? Marianne laughingly replied, "I just want to keep my truck running. I want to grow from 1,100 to 2,000 gallons because right now it's just me." She self-distributes to Boulder liquor stores, sells at farmers' markets, and by the glass at the Nomad Theatre in Boulder. She thinks being at the markets where people can meet and buy from the winemaker has an impact on sales.

Visit Boulder some weekend and enjoy both Marianne's wine and her enthusiasm for life.

WINE LIST

Harvest Gold
Joie de Vino Chardonnay
Ruby (Cabernet Franc and Ruby Cabernet blend)
WineChick Blues (Merlot and Cabernet Sauvignon blend)
WineChick Red (Lemberger)
WineChick White (Riesling)

Avanti Winery

OWNER'S NAME: Jim "Griff" Griffin
WINEMAKER: Jim Griffin
YEAR LICENSED: 2001
ADDRESS: 9046 W. Bowles Ave. #H, Littleton, Colorado 80123
TELEPHONE: 303-904-7650
WEBSITE: N/A
TASTING ROOM HOURS: 11 A.M.–7 P.M. Thursday–Friday; 10 A.M.–6 P.M. Saturday; 11 A.M.–5 P.M. Sunday
WINE AVAILABILITY OUTSIDE WINERY: No
PRICE RANGE OF WINES SOLD AT WINERY: $8.00–$28.00 for all Colorado wines, including Avanti
WINE CLUB: No
ANNUAL PRODUCTION: 90 gallons of Port, available December 2002

DIRECTIONS TO THE WINERY: Near Southwest Plaza in Arapahoe County. Take Wadsworth south of Hampden (Highway 285) to Bowles, west on Bowles just past Southwest Plaza. The winery is on the south side just past Flower Street. The winery is under the auspices of the Gars and Grapes store.

FACILITIES AND AMENITIES: A large selection of other Colorado wines for tasting and purchase, plus wine accessories and a walk-in humidor with an extensive selection of cigars.

Jim Griffin has expanded his cigar store to include a tasting room and sales of Colorado wines, but he also has a winery license. His own wines, using Colorado grapes, are expected to be released in December 2002, beginning with his Port-style. Next will be a Chardonnay and Merlot.

We are anxious to see the bottles with his Avanti label, a gold foil "A" with a rose inside it. The name for the winery came from his silent partner and companion—his dog, Avanti. As of January 2002, he had eleven Colorado wineries represented in the store and was planning to carry more.

WINES REPRESENTED

Avanti Winery
Bookcliff Vineyards
Canyon Wind Cellars
Carlson Cellars
Cottonwood Cellars
Creekside Cellars
Grande River Vineyards
Old Town Winery
Plum Creek Cellars
S. Rhodes Cellars
Trail Ridge Winery
Two Rivers Winery

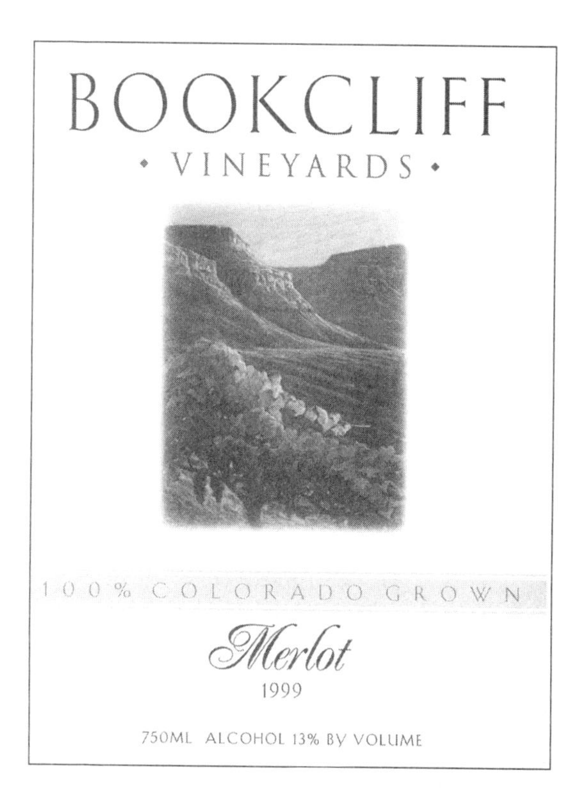

Bookcliff Vineyards

OWNERS' NAMES: John Garlich and Ulla Merz
WINEMAKER: John Garlich
YEAR LICENSED: 1999
ADDRESS: N/A
TELEPHONE: 303-499-7301
WEBSITE: www.bookcliffvineyards.net
TASTING ROOM HOURS: None
WINE AVAILABILITY OUTSIDE WINERY: Boulder Farmers Market, Chautauqua Dining Hall, Avanti Winery (see separate listing), some Boulder liquor stores.
PRICE RANGE OF WINES: $12.00–$14.00
WINE CLUB: No
ANNUAL PRODUCTION: 2,800–3,500 gallons

DIRECTIONS TO THE BOULDER FARMERS MARKET: On 13th Street between Arapahoe and Canyon near downtown Boulder. The market is open from 8 A.M.–2 P.M. on Saturdays from April to the end of October.

FACILITIES AND AMENITIES: N/A

Sometimes a little wine-tasting can get out of hand. Ask John Garlich, who with his wife, Ulla Merz, and some friends started putting together regular wine-tasting parties in the 1970s. One thing led to another, with "the other" being John making small quantities of wine from grapes he had shipped to his home in Boulder.

Garlich still makes wine in the basement of the couple's home in southeast Boulder near the University of Colorado president's house. But this has gone well beyond the hobby stage, as he made 350 cases in 1999, 900 cases in 2000 and expected to have 1,500 cases out of his 2001 harvest. The basement of his home is filled with fermentation and storage tanks, oak barrels, cardboard cases, wine racks and other accoutrements of the trade.

Garlich's output is one of the reasons to go to the Boulder Farmers Market on Saturdays from spring to fall. That's one of the best places to find his wine, as well as the wine from Augustina's Winery, because they share a booth. You can't, however, taste the wine before buying it. The farmers market was his only outlet, other than his friends, until 2001 when he started marketing to some Boulder restaurants and liquor stores.

Garlich is a structural engineer by training and salesman for a pre-stress concrete company by occupation. He met his wife, a German native who is a computing consultant, when they both came to Boulder in the 1970s. The wine-tasting parties got Garlich thinking about starting a winery and the couple even looked at Oregon property.

In the early 1980s, they discovered Colorado wine while on a bike trip to Moab, Utah, where a winery owner told them some wineries were opening in their own state. In 1995, they bought 10 acres of land in the Vinelands area of Palisade at the mouth of DeBeque Canyon. Garlich has an old photograph, taken about 1900, that shows vines on the property, vines that were ripped out during Prohibition.

They now have Chardonnay, Merlot, Cabernet Sauvignon, Viognier, Cabernet Franc and black Muscat grapes. Garlich doesn't use all of their harvest, selling what he can't use to other winemakers. Like many other winemakers, he learned his skills by taking classes through the University of California at Davis and reading books on vineyard management and oenology.

The wine that Garlich hopes to become known for is a blend akin to the red wines of the Bordeaux region of France, using Cabernet Sauvignon, Cabernet Franc and Merlot. It's a blend similar to what some U.S. wineries call a Meritage, but which Garlich calls his "Ensemble" wine.

Garlich also makes a Chardonnay that is aged in a French style called *sur lees,* which means fermenting and aging on the yeast solids instead of filtering them off. It's a process that produces wines that are less prone to oxidation and generally taste softer but with more flavor.

WINE LIST

Chardonnay
Ensemble
Merlot
Viognier

Creekside Cellars

OWNER'S NAME: William F. Donahue
WINEMAKER: William F. Donahue
YEAR LICENSED: 1996
ADDRESS: 28036 Highway 74, Evergreen, Colorado 80439
TELEPHONE: 303-674-5460
WEBSITE: N/A
TASTING ROOM HOURS: Wednesday–Sunday, 11 A.M.–5 P.M.
WINE AVAILABILITY OUTSIDE WINERY: Selected restaurants
PRICE RANGE OF WINES SOLD AT WINERY: $8.00–$24.00
WINE CLUB: No

ANNUAL PRODUCTION: 4,000 gallons

DIRECTIONS TO THE WINERY: Located in downtown Evergreen on the Bear Creek (south) side of Highway 74.

FACILITIES AND AMENITIES: The tasting room is part of an Italian-style delicatessen, featuring hot and cold sandwiches, soup, salad and a few desserts. The bathrooms may be the best in any public facility in the state.

You have to be ready for plenty of interruptions if you sit with Bill Donahue at one of the tables in front of Creekside Cellars in Evergreen. The problem is not that everyone seems to know Bill; they seem to genuinely like him. One day when we were interviewing him, people kept stopping by to shake hands and give him presents. One friend stopped by with some antique French wine bottles. A chef from a restaurant down the street came by to compliment him on his deli sandwiches and to buy his lunch.

Donahue needs some good fortune with his winery; it has taken him longer than anyone could have imagined to get it open. When we wrote the first edition of our book in 1997, he thought he would be open about six months later. Licensed in 1996, that didn't seem too much of a stretch. But Creekside Cellars didn't open until November 26, 2000. The biggest reason it took so long was that the site Donahue purchased for the winery, otherwise a great location in the heart of well-traveled Evergreen, had been a gasoline station for a number of years. It also had been vacant for a long time.

Donahue learned a hard lesson about the environmental and governmental issues involved in converting a former gas station into a food and beverage establishment. He had to spend thousands of dollars on environmental studies, let alone the construction that was necessary. In order to build a cantilevered deck in the back over Bear Creek he had to pay for a 24-month study to satisfy federal concerns about what would happen if there were a 100-year flood.

By March of 2000, after suffering a bad car accident, Donahue was ready to give up. But his son, Tim, who had graduated from college a year earlier, convinced him to keep going. Tim said he would help manage the delicatessen and winery, as well help in the renovation.

Donahue, who owned a family printing business in Arvada, originally wanted a winery in the Palisade area. He decided to stay in the Denver area because that is where his extended family lives.

Donahue blames his wife, Anita, and grandmother for getting him interested in making wine. Anita, his high school sweetheart, comes from an Italian family, and Donahue says he started drinking wine at her family dinners. His grandmother gave him a wine-making kit in the 1970s and he started making wine from grapes soon after.

"Those first grapes I bought (California Zinfandel) were so good you couldn't screw them up," he says. "They made you think you were a winemaker overnight."

Donahue concentrates on making small batches of wine, about 200 gallons at a time. He makes a red table wine called Rosso ("red" in Italian) that can be a blend of different grapes—a recent vintage was Merlot and Cabernet Franc—and a white named Bianco ("white") that also is a blend, but was mostly Gewürztraminer when we had it. One distinctive recent offering is his LakeHaus Port, made from black Muscat grapes.

Inside the deli/tasting room are six wood tables with chairs where you can enjoy a glass of wine and deli items like focaccia and pannini made with eggplant, Portobello mushrooms, roasted red peppers and prosciutto. Daily specials may include a concoction called Strombolo, a rolled pizza crust stuffed with veggies or meats. On Saturdays you may find entertainment, a small band or soloist, playing for a few hours in the afternoon. It's easy to see why the place is crowded on weekends.

WINE LIST

Bianco
Cabernet Franc
Chardonnay
LakeHaus Port Black Muscat
Merlot
Pinot Noir
Riesling Port
Rosato (a Rosé blend)

J. A. Balistreri Vineyards

OWNERS' NAMES: John and Birdie Balistreri and daughter, Julie Balistreri
WINEMAKER: John Balistreri
YEAR LICENSED: 1998
ADDRESS: 1946 E. 66th Avenue, Denver, Colorado 80229
TELEPHONE: 303-287-5156

WEBSITE: N/A
TASTING ROOM HOURS: 1 P.M.–5 P.M. Saturdays or by appointment
WINE AVAILABILITY OUTSIDE WINERY: Liquor stores in the Denver area and at Three Sons Italian restaurant and the Sambucca Jazz Cafe
PRICE RANGE OF WINES SOLD AT WINERY: $16.00–$24.00
WINE CLUB: Yes
ANNUAL PRODUCTION: 2,400 gallons
DIRECTIONS TO THE WINERY: Take I-25 to 58th Avenue Exit and go east to Washington Street. Turn left (north) on 66th Avenue, go east on 66th Avenue 0.75 mile to winery on your right.
FACILITIES AND AMENITIES: Tasting room, fresh flower bouquets, gift baskets, and the winery is available for wine and cheese parties.

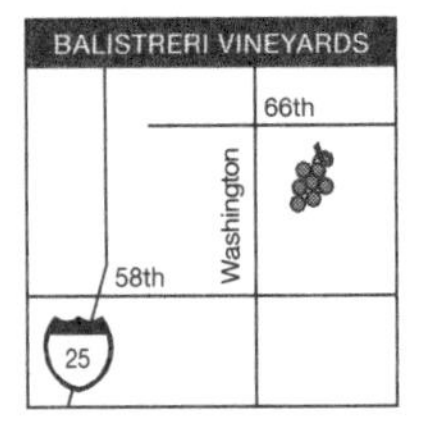

You might find it hard to believe there is a vineyard and winery in the midst of industrial parks and warehouses in the Denver area, but there is—a 15-acre oasis where generations of Balistreris have lived and worked. The grandparents came from Palermo, Sicily, and began with truck farming. Then in 1965, they built greenhouses, selling wholesale cut flowers to places like Alfalfa's. Since 1998, when J. A. Balistreri's Vineyards opened, they have also been raising grapes and making wine. Flowers and wine may seem unrelated, but John Balistreri says it was a natural progression. "I've been around wine since I was a kid; my uncles all made homemade wine. I started making red wine in 1991 at home for my family."

The entire Balistreri family is involved with the winery, John as winemaker, Birdie cleaning and working in the tasting room and arranging flowers for Saturday's business, and daughter Julie, who works closely with her father making wine decisions and taking care of ordering grapes, marketing and distribution. No matter whom you meet in the tasting room, you will be greeted with a warm smile by a person who is happy in their job.

Many would say they are crazy to grow grapes. Denver's weather and climate are all wrong—too cold in winter—for successful grape-growing. But the Balistreris hope to have conquered that problem with an underground water system from Grow Air Co., which is not only an efficient way to water, but also is hooked up to an air compressor. Through it they can re-aerate the soil after watering or push warm air through it to raise the air temperature from the ground up. Their own addition to the system is a polyethylene canopy over the grape trellises, which can be dropped to protect the grapes from freezing winds.

"Planting costs us about $14,000 an acre because of all these extras," John says, about $4,000 more than the usual cost of planting. Julie explained, "Water shuts down a plant, so giving them oxygen encourages growth and speeds up crop time."

The Balistreris also sought help from international wine consultant Dr. Richard Smart of Australia, who advised them to let the young shoots grow through the grape canopy and then bury the young canes, saving the young vines in the event of a hard freeze. Has all this time and expense been worth it? In 2000, they harvested 6.5 tons of Cabernet Sauvignon and Merlot on their 4 acres and the 0.25 acre of Muscat looked good in 2001, plenty to share with John's brother-in-law, Clyde Spero (see related story on Spero Winery). Asked why they would go to these lengths, Julie answered, "For love of the grape."

When they began making wine for the winery, they had to order some of their grapes from California. Keeping it in the family, they bought grapes from a cousin in Lodi, who shipped their grapes in refrigerated trucks only twenty hours after picking. In 2001, however, they used 75 percent Colorado grapes (seven barrels of their grapes and forty-one barrels purchased from other Colorado growers). They were worried about the sugar levels of their grapes picked in September 2000, but John said the grapes were perfect.

The Balistreris also have an uncommon natural approach to their unfiltered wines, beginning with 1,000 pounds at a time sitting in a barrel, fermenting with their stems and husks on to produce natural tannins that prevent oxidizing. They add no sulfites or other chemicals. John says they do little adjusting. "It's all in the grape," he says.

He believes each barrel of wine is unique; therefore, their wine bottles are numbered according to the barrel. If you love the wine you just tasted, you'll need to buy more then because although the differences will be minimal, the wine from another barrel might not be exactly the same. Julie says: "It's more work to do each individual barrel, but we think it's important. We leave everything at least eleven months on oak."

Their newly constructed tasting room/cellar/winery is four blocks east of their vineyard. The cellar provides an even temperature for year-round storage.

Going up the walk to the winery, you can see the greenhouses down the hill where the family works at their "real" jobs. Inside, you'll be greeted by fresh flower bouquets and get your first look at their labels, which appropriately pictures barrels in a wine cellar and whose top has white wax artfully dripping down the bottle instead of the more common foil.

WINE LIST

Cabernet Sauvignon
Merlot
Muscat
Petite Syrah
Sangiovese
Semillon Chardonnay
Zinfandel

Fruit Wines

Cherry

Old Town Winery

OWNERS' NAMES: Conrad and Mary Rose Kindsfather
WINEMAKER: Conrad Kindsfather
YEAR LICENSED: 1997 (relicensed 2001)
ADDRESS: 5659 Old Wadsworth, Arvada, Colorado 80002-2532
TELEPHONE: 888-990-WINE (9463)
WEBSITE: www.oldtownwinery.com
TASTING ROOM HOURS: Call for hours
WINE AVAILABILITY OUTSIDE WINERY: Self-distributed to some liquor stores in Denver–Boulder area.
PRICE RANGE OF WINES SOLD AT WINERY: N/A
WINE CLUB: No
ANNUAL PRODUCTION: 1,500 gallons

DIRECTIONS TO THE WINERY: Entrance to the winery is from the alley on the west side of the building off Old Wadsworth in the Old Arvada area.

FACILITIES AND AMENITIES: Tasting area

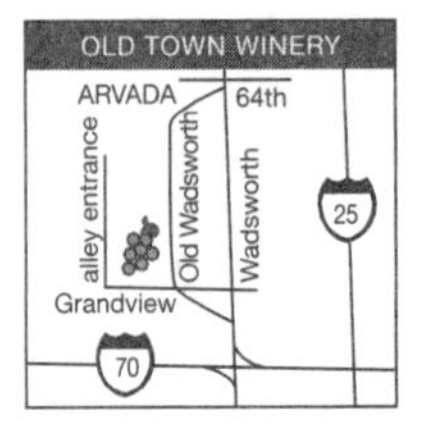

Old Town Winery has had kind of a funky character since it was opened by Randy Zeleny in 1997. But Zeleny, who ran a successful Volkswagen parts store next door, sold both businesses in August 2001, with the winery purchased by Conrad Kindsfather.

Kindsfather, whose law firm Kindsfather & Associates is next door to the building housing the winery, plans initially to keep Old Town Winery operating in the same location and producing the same kinds of wines. In the future he may offer premium wines under another label.

Kindsfather bought the winery because he has been making his own wine for a number of years and says he is fascinated with the process. When Zeleny decided to sell out and take an extended vacation, Kindsfather jumped at the chance. He's going to continue to practice law, although his caseload likely will go down.

Since he bought the winery just before the fall harvest in 2001, Kindsfather got involved in wine-making quickly, buying grapes from Western Slope growers to crush, ferment and bottle for his first wine production.

WINE LIST (from previous owner)

Cabernet Franc
Chardonnay
Gewürztraminer
Merlot
Pinot Noir
Sauvignon Blanc
Semillon
The Edge Red (blend of Merlot and Semillon)
The Edge White (blend of Sauvignon Blanc and Semillon)

Pikes Peak Vineyards

OWNERS' NAMES: Mac Gray, Bruce and Taffy McLaughlin
WINEMAKER: Paul Tafoya
YEAR LICENSED: 1981
ADDRESS: 3900 Janitell Road, Colorado Springs, Colorado 80906
TELEPHONE: 719-576-0075
WEBSITE: N/A
TASTING ROOM HOURS: 1 P.M.–4 P.M. daily
WINE AVAILABILITY OUTSIDE WINERY: At the store Wines of Colorado, Cascade, Colorado
PRICE RANGE OF WINES SOLD AT WINERY: $10.00–$12.00
WINE CLUB: No
ANNUAL PRODUCTION: 5,000–10,000 gallons

DIRECTIONS TO THE WINERY: Take I-25 to Colorado Springs and get off at Exit 138. Go east on Circle Drive to the Second Janitell Road, turn right and continue south on Janitell for a half-mile. Pikes Peak will be on your left.

FACILITIES AND AMENITIES: Restaurant, tasting room, 9-hole golf course and driving range

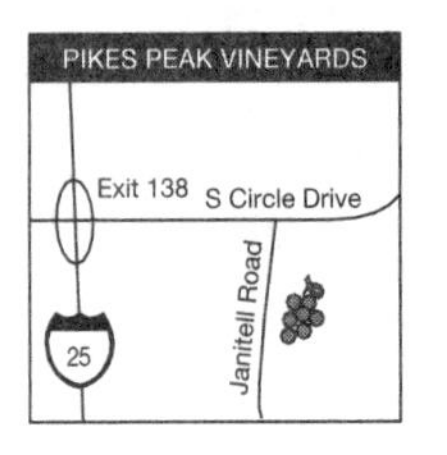

Within close proximity though not truly visible from I-25 is Pikes Peak Vineyards, which sits on a 100-acre estate in the southern end of Colorado Springs. Originally part of the 1862 Bates ranch homestead, it later became the site of the old Sinton Dairy. The winery/restaurant building was Jim Sinton's home, restored in the 1950s with cork walls to keep the building cool in summer and warm in winter.

Since its early beginnings, the estate has seen many changes. It now has a public 9-hole regulation golf course and driving range called the Vineyards Golf Course, open since 1999, possibly because part owner Bruce McLaughlin plays a lot of golf and he thought Colorado Springs needed another golf course. McLaughlin also runs the Minturn Cellars winery near Vail, dividing his time between the two.

The land is home to 600 Chandler grape vines from New York, which are planted next to the golf course. They are resistant to cold, but, of course, not the hail that often hits the area. They were expected to produce their first crop in 2002, but Paul Tafoya, winemaker and vineyard manager, says they are uncertain what they will do with them.

A restaurant, most recently named the "Red Cedar Grill" and serving what Bruce calls American food and Pikes Peak wine, is located on the first floor of the homestead, and has been leased to various tenants. Below the restaurant on the west side is the winery entrance. A small wine press and barrels may be outside when you arrive.

Bruce says he is no longer the winemaker, turning that job over to Paul Tafoya, who says he "does a little bit of everything." The tasting room is not apparent as you walk in the front door. You'll be looking at fermentation/storage tanks, but Paul is usually around and will take you to a tasting area with a bar that used to be upstairs in the restaurant when the tasting room was part of the restaurant space.

Bruce has experimented with many grapes in his winemaking,

buying from growers in Colorado, including Cayuga grapes from Pueblo County that were in the tanks when we visited.

While sitting at the bar in the tasting room, you may notice labels on bottles, such as "Spirit of the Bayonet," a label made for a general at Fort Carson Army Base. Pikes Peak has made custom labels for their wine for individuals who wanted them for a special occasion.

WINE LIST

Cabernet Franc
Cabernet Sauvignon
Chardonnay
Coyote White (a sweet Sauvignon Blanc)
Merlot
Riesling
Sauvignon Blanc
Semillon
Virgin Blush
Zeb's Red (a sweet Merlot)

Redstone Meadery

OWNER'S NAME: David Myers
MEAD MAKER: David Myers
YEAR LICENSED: 2000
ADDRESS: 4700 Pearl Street, Unit 2A, Boulder, Colorado 80301
TELEPHONE: 720-406-1215
WEBSITE: www.redstonemeadery.com
TASTING ROOM HOURS: By appointment; please check for newly established hours.
MEAD AVAILABILITY OUTSIDE WINERY: Local restaurants
PRICE RANGE OF WINES SOLD AT WINERY: Check for pricing at the Meadery on their half-gallon jugs, large and small kegs, all "to go."

MEAD CLUB: No
ANNUAL PRODUCTION: 2,000–3,000 gallons
DIRECTIONS TO THE WINERY: Take U.S. Highway 36 to Foothills Parkway to Pearl, turn right at Pearl and take an immediate left on 47th. Take a right on Old Pearl, and the meadery is directly on your right.
FACILITIES AND AMENITIES: Tastings and tours by appointment only

David Myers grew up in Baltimore, and when he graduated from college he wanted to work at a ski resort. His mother suggested Vail and off he went. After growing tired of Vail, he moved to Boulder and ran a T-shirt factory. He became attached to the brewers' association and started home brewing in 1990. This led him to a meeting with Paul Gatza, the director of the association, who happened to make mead, which was so good it inspired David to try his hand.

David found out that making mead was not going to be that easy. In researching mead around the country, he found a lot of differences in the twenty or so meaderies in existence in the late 1990s. Even licensing was a problem; the Federal Bureau of Alcohol, Tobacco and Firearms didn't know whether to license him as a winery or a brewery. According to his research, mead is a wine and some can be saved for years—he had one from Poland that was twenty-five years old.

Myers was not deterred. "I want to be part of bringing back the history and culture of mead," he says. "We need more meaderies to become an industry." He sought the help of Brian Lutz, head brewer at Redfish Brewing Co. in Boulder, to assess equipment and for training.

Mead, a fermented honey wine, has a long tradition; think Beowulf and Vikings. David told us the word "honeymoon" comes from the tradition of drinking honey wine for thirty days after marriage. He admits that mead requires educating the consumer. That's why he wanted to do it in Boulder because he feels the population there is more open to new things.

His goal is to make regular mead (12 percent alcohol) and also add other flavors. He has plans for a bottled vintage reserve mead that has a longer shelf life and a higher alcohol content. Presently, he says, "I've created 'nectar,' making it sparkling by adding carbon dioxide and black raspberry puree. It's force-carbonated and fruited, served cold, about 40 to 45 degrees."

He thinks his market is the twenty-one- to thirty-year-old group, slanted more toward women who like wine and fruit and something that's light and refreshing.

David uses local honey, initially from Madhava Honey of Lyons, which is convenient enough to go and pick up, but orders his fruit puree from the Oregon Fruit Company. This is a one-man operation and his own invention. "I'm not aware of anyone else using pasteurization and temperature-controlled fermentation," he ventures.

The mead is currently available at the Redstone Meadery or on tap at some local restaurants. If you get the chance, look at the beautiful tap handles on his commercial kegs; the eye-catching design was done by local artist Jen Thario.

David says he's positioned for the long haul, a three- to four-year start-up. He has a wealth of ideas for the future of his meads, including something different to personalize one's wedding. He plans to tie mead to weddings and the whole honeymoon tradition with the general marketing plan to make bottles with private labels.

MEAD LIST

Black Raspberry Nectar
Boysenberry Nectar

Trail Ridge Winery

OWNERS' NAMES: Tim Merrick, Mark Fiore, Ron Binz, Wes Melander, Howard Golden

WINEMAKER: Tim Merrick

YEAR LICENSED: 1995

ADDRESS: 4113 W. Eisenhower Blvd. (U.S. Highway 34), Loveland, Colorado 80537

TELEPHONE: 970-635-0949

WEBSITE: www.trailridgewinery.com

TASTING ROOM HOURS: March–April, 10 A.M.–5 P.M. Wednesday–Sunday; May–December, 10 A.M.–5:30 P.M. daily

WINE AVAILABILITY OUTSIDE WINERY: Statewide distribution, predominantly Front Range liquor stores, many mountain resorts and several restaurants. Ship to reciprocal states.

PRICE RANGE OF WINES SOLD AT WINERY: $9.00–$14.00

WINE CLUB: No
ANNUAL PRODUCTION: 6,000 gallons
DIRECTIONS TO THE WINERY: Take I-25 north to Exit 257B and drive 7 miles west on U.S. Highway 34. The winery's on your right, just past where there is a fork in the road.
FACILITIES AND AMENITIES: Tasting room, picnic tables, deck.

If you feel life is too fast-paced, take a drive to Loveland and leave the "rat race" behind at Trail Ridge Winery. This had been the Mattoon family farm, founded at the turn of the century where they planted thirty varieties of apple trees. The orchard is no longer apparent, but you'll see grape vines planted near the winery.

Tim Merrick and his partners bought the 8-acre farm in 1992 and opened the winery in 1995. Tim's interest in wine-making goes back fifteen years before that, when he graduated from the University of Colorado and headed to San Francisco where he was introduced to "good wine." He lived in the North Beach area and "there was an old guy who lived in an apartment in the basement who made his own wine, including crushing the grapes," Tim tells us. That Zinfandel sparked his wine-making interest, and in 1986, he began North Denver Cellars in Denver, which served beer and wine-making hobbyists.

Merrick's wine-making enthusiasm has not waned. His production increased so much in the last five years that they may need to build a warehouse in back of the winery, especially since some of his red wine is not bottled for a year. One of his reds, Lemberger, is not a common grape in Colorado. Tim says, "For me as a winemaker, it's been fun to work with a wine that's not so well known. Washington state knows it, and it's fun to have someone (from Washington) come in (and taste) and compare it to theirs back home."

Part of the customer's fun has to be meeting the winemaker, Tim, with his easy manner and his laid-back style. It could be the reason they sell more than half of their wine from the tasting room alone. In spite of Tim's leanings toward Alsatian wines and the Lemberger, Trail Ridge still offers a wide variety of wines. Tim believes Lemberger could be Colorado's signature wine, adding "I'm biased toward Alsatian wines. We'll probably get into Pinot Gris."

Tim buys his grapes from Colorado growers and has formed long-term relationships with them. He has such a strong relationship with his growers that one talked to Tim before planting. Tim says, "There's been more press and public recognition (of the Colorado wine industry), and this has spawned a number of people getting in the 'business'—all levels—growers, winemakers, Front

Range investors, even a new vineyard management company, Hernandez." Tim would prefer to have more neighboring wineries to make this area a wine region, more of a "destination."

It can be your destination, though. Stay in the area, have dinner or pack a picnic and bring the kids if you want. Trail Ridge also carries Monrico's ciders (non-alcoholic). Slow down, breathe some fresh air and enjoy Tim's wine.

If you go to Trail Ridge Winery and want a weekend getaway, consider staying at the nearby Wild Lane Bed & Breakfast Inn, nestled in an old grove of trees with access to hiking trails. The inn has five rooms and serves a full breakfast. It is located at 5445 Wild Lane west of the winery; 970-669-0303 or 800-204-3320.

WINE LIST

Cabernet Franc
Chardonnay
Fall River Red
Gewürztraminer
Lemberger
Merlot
Never Summer White
Prairie Rose
Riesling

OPENING SOON

Spero Winery

OWNERS' NAMES: Clyde and June Spero
WINEMAKER: Clyde Spero
YEAR LICENSED: 1999
ADDRESS: N/A
TELEPHONE: 303-428-9830
WEBSITE: N/A
TASTING ROOM HOURS: Watch for opening
WINE AVAILABILITY OUTSIDE WINERY: N/A
PRICE RANGE OF WINES SOLD AT WINERY: N/A
WINE CLUB: No
ANNUAL PRODUCTION IN GALLONS: N/A
DIRECTIONS TO THE WINERY: Watch for a north or northwest Denver address
FACILITIES AND AMENITIES: N/A

The Spero Winery, named for its owners, should be called the "midnight winery," according to June Spero, because that is when they do all their winery work. The owners aren't new at wine-making, even though they set a spring 2002 opening. Clyde Spero learned wine-making from his father, who came from "the old country," and he has continually made wines at home for many years that have pleased both family and friends.

Clyde's wife, June, is a Balistreri, and the two families share the grapes planted at 66th Avenue and Washington Street in north Denver. Yet, June says, "Our wines will be a different style than my brother's (John Balistreri). It's like two cooks making spaghetti sauce. They're never the same."

The Speros will be making full-bodied, rich wines in the tradition of European wines. They are putting everything in American oak barrels for two years.

Watch for their first label, "Vino è Buono" ("wine is good" in Italian). In spite of having "day jobs," they started with 100 barrels filled with wine, enabling them to open with a good supply of quality wine.

A winery has been a long dream of the Speros. June never tires of reminding her husband that back in the 1980s when the oil industry was going "belly-up," June suggested buying land on the Western Slope, planting grapes, and having a winery when they retired. "You're crazy!" Clyde said, "Nobody grows grapes there!" Oh well—now part of that vision is coming into fruition, just in a different place.

WINE LIST (at opening)

Cabernet Sauvignon
Merlot
Shiraz
Zinfandel

WATCH FOR

Blue Mountain Winery

Bill Prewitt planted 5 acres of wine grapes in 1999 in the Little Thompson River Valley near Berthoud with the intention of starting a winery in the future. He is getting help from his son, Brian, a brewer at Great Divide Brewery in Denver. Brian says the grapes are primarily *Vitis vinifera* and not hybrids.

The Winery at Holy Cross Abbey

It seems both historically and culturally appropriate that the Benedictine Monks should have a winery in Cañon City. Historically, because wine grapes were grown at the mouth of the Arkansas River Canyon more than a century ago. Culturally, because the order is famous for its Benedictine liqueur.

The Holy Cross Abbey, which is run by the Benedictines on the east side of Cañon City, has big plans for wine grapes. In 2001, the order hired a former Colorado winemaker, Matt Cookson, as a consultant and planted 1 acre of Chardonnay grapes. More vines are planned as well as a wine-tasting room (tasting wines from elsewhere) at the abbey in the summer of 2002.

The abbey plans on opening a winery in 2003, according to Father Gregory Legge, the abbey's chief financial officer. It will be called The Winery at Holy Cross Abbey.

The story behind the abbey's interest in wine-making is appropriately religious. It began with a 1999 visit that one member of the order, Father Paul Montez, paid to Fred Strothman, the owner of Rocky Mountain Meadery and St. Kathryn Cellars in Palisade. Strothman told Father Montez he was having a lot of trouble getting St. Kathryn Cellars opened and asked the father to bless the winery. After the father's blessing, Strothman encouraged the abbey to think about growing grapes and making wine. Strothman, who joined the abbey's board, helped the abbey contract with Cookson, who had moved to California's wine region after Denver's Columbine Cellars closed in 1997.

Father Legge says the abbey, founded in 1923, wants the winery to become a travel destination, eventually adding a restaurant, a museum and an arts and crafts center. All the income from the operation will go to further the abbey's educational mission.

Will the abbey make Benedictine liqueur? Probably not for some time, says Father Legge, but it is a wine-related product so that may happen. Meanwhile, the abbey may foster renewed interest in grape-growing and wine-making in the Arkansas River Valley. The Colorado Department of Corrections already has planted thousands of wine grape vines in the valley for sale to wineries.

RECIPES FROM THE WINERIES

APPETIZERS/BEVERAGES

GARFIELD ESTATES WINERY'S WHITE SANGRIA

Ingredients

2 bottles of Garfield Estates' Sauvignon Blanc
¼ cup Grand Marnier
2 tablespoons sugar
¼ cup seedless red grapes, halved
¼ cup seedless green grapes, halved
5 orange slices, halved
½ Red Delicious apple, unpeeled, cored and sliced thinly

Method

In a pitcher combine the wine, Grand Marnier and sugar and stir the mixture. Add the grapes, orange slices and apple slices and chill the sangria, stirring occasionally, for 2 hours. The sangria may be made up to 24 hours in advance and kept covered and chilled.

"Serve this festive beverage in a clear glass pitcher and pour in wineglasses with a wedge of marinated fruit from the pitcher. Play a little Ottmar Liebert in the background and you are transported to Barcelona, Spain!" —*Carol Carr*

Alta's Notes: I made this 3½ hours before serving and when it was served to four couples, some expressed how much they liked it, despite the fact they dislike red wine-based Sangria. It was pretty and light, and the wine-soaked fruit was an added treat.

Recipe provided by Carol Carr

GARFIELD ESTATES' ROASTED ALMONDS

Ingredients

4 cups raw, whole almonds, skin on
2 tablespoons fresh rosemary
½ teaspoon crushed red pepper flakes
1 teaspoon lemon juice
1 teaspoon salt
Black pepper to taste
½ cup extra virgin olive oil

Method

Dry roast almonds in 400-degree oven until slightly smoking (approximately 10 to 15 minutes). Add almonds to all the remaining ingredients, tossing periodically until cool.

Alta's Notes: The almonds need to be cooked early in the day and allowed to cool completely. These are good roasted, subtly flavored almonds made with a healthy oil, but we love the taste of rosemary and would probably add more. There is an abundant amount of olive oil, so I suggest you drain the almonds on paper towels before serving. Adjust spices/herbs to your individual taste and enjoy this easy appetizer/snack.

Recipe provided by Carol Carr

GRAYSTONE WINERY'S SCALLOP APPETIZER (SOUP)

Ingredients

2 tablespoons butter
1 pound scallops, small
10 mushroom caps
1 tablespoon fresh ginger, grated
⅔ cup Graystone Vineyard's Pinot Gris
1 tablespoon fresh lemon juice
1 cup whipping cream
Salt and freshly ground pepper
1 tablespoon Parmesan cheese, grated

Method

Melt butter over medium heat. Add scallops, mushrooms and ginger and sauté for 2 minutes. Transfer mushrooms and scallops to platter and set aside. Add wine and lemon juice to skillet. Cook until liquid is reduced by half. Blend in cream and cook until reduced by half again. Add mushrooms and scallops and salt and pepper. Cook until just heated through. Sprinkle with Parmesan cheese. Transfer to broiler and broil until lightly browned. Serve in four small soup bowls with sourdough bread as a first course.

Alta's Notes: What a delightful flavor combination. It's a very creamy, easy soup.

Recipe provided by Barbara Maurer

SALADS

MOUNTAIN SPIRIT WINERY'S GREEK SALAD WITH GRILLED CHICKEN BREASTS

Ingredients

2 boneless, skinless chicken breasts
Bite-size pieced assorted salad greens
2 medium green onions, sliced
Feta cheese, crumbled
12 Kalamata or any large, pitted ripe olives
1 medium tomato, coarsely chopped
½ cucumber, coarsely chopped

Method

Prepare the lemon vinaigrette (see recipe on page 151).

Grill chicken breasts either on the barbecue or in the broiler. "It's better on the grill." Place salad greens, onions, feta cheese, olives, tomato and cucumber on the plates. Slice chicken breasts and place on top of the salad. Pour lemon vinaigrette over all.

Serves 2

Alta's Notes: Personal preference—I peeled and seeded the cucumber and put just a little vinaigrette on the breasts before grilling. This is a light, refreshing meal.

Recipe provided by Terri Barkett

LEMON VINAIGRETTE

Ingredients

¼ cup olive or vegetable oil
2 tablespoon lemon juice
½ teaspoon salt and pepper to taste
1 small clove garlic, finely chopped
1 tablespoon fresh oregano, chopped or 1 teaspoon dry oregano

Method

Shake all ingredients in tightly covered container. Serve with French bread or rolls.

"While Michael and I were testing the Blackberry Chardonnay blend, we had some in a lab bottle, unfiltered and unfinished. We were enjoying this meal and tried the raw Blackberry/ Chardonnay with it. We decided that it made this salad even better. Prepare this great salad for just the two of you and have a wonderful romantic evening." —*Terri Barkett*

SURFACE CREEK WINERY'S GRILLED CHICKEN SALAD

Ingredients

3 skinless, boneless chicken breast halves
6 to 8 cups torn leaf lettuce
6 to 8 cherry tomatoes, quartered
1 small, sweet red pepper, halved and seeded
1 cup croutons

Dressing:

¼ cup olive oil
2 tablespoons lemon juice
1 teaspoon sugar
1 teaspoon dry oregano
Black pepper, freshly ground
2 tablespoons mayonnaise
1 tablespoon Parmesan cheese, finely grated

Method

Preheat broiler or grill.

Prepare dressing: Whisk together olive oil, lemon juice, sugar, oregano, pepper and mayonnaise. Drizzle 2 tablespoons over chicken. Then add grated Parmesan cheese to remaining dressing. Make salad from lettuce and cherry tomatoes. Toss with dressing.

Grill chicken 3 to 4 minutes per side or until no longer pink. Grill sweet red peppers about 2 minutes per side.

Slice chicken breasts diagonally and place on individual portions of salad on each plate. Top with croutons. Thinly slice grilled red pepper and place decoratively on the side of the plate.

Serve with Surface Creek Winery's Chenin Blanc.

Serves 3

Alta's Notes: What a nice and easy spring or summer meal. The dressing is thick but light, and the red pepper is a tasty addition.

Recipe provided by Jeanne Durr

ENTREES

ASPEN VALLEY WINERY'S PIZZA ON THE GRILL

Ingredients

1 cup warm water
1 envelope active dry yeast
1 teaspoon sugar
2 teaspoons (Kosher or sea) salt
3 tablespoons cornmeal
3 tablespoons whole wheat flour
1 tablespoon extra virgin olive oil, plus oil for the bowl, the baking sheet and brushing pizza crust
3 to 3½ cups unbleached all-purpose flour, or as needed
Pizza cheese
Pizza sauce, canned or homemade
Toppings as desired, such as fresh basil leaves, sun-dried tomatoes in oil (drained) or goat cheese

Method

Place water in a large bowl and add the yeast and sugar. Stir to dissolve and let sit 5 minutes. Stir in salt, cornmeal, whole wheat flour and oil. Gradually stir in enough all-purpose flour to form a dough that comes away from the sides of the bowl. Knead the dough on a floured work surface, or in a food processor or mixer fitted with a dough hook until smooth and elastic. The dough should be soft and pliable, but not sticky. Kneading should take 6 to 8 minutes.

Lightly oil a clean large bowl. Place the dough in the bowl, brush the top with oil, and cover loosely with plastic wrap. Let the dough rise in a warm, draft-free spot until doubled in bulk, 1 to 2 hours. Punch down the dough. Let the dough rise until doubled in bulk again, 40 to 50 minutes. Punch it down again. Divide the dough into two equal pieces, shaping each into a ball.

Preheat grill so that one side is on high and one is on medium. If using charcoal, set it up for two-tiered grilling, arranging the coals in a double layer on one side and in a single layer on the other.

(recipe cont. on next page)

Generously oil a large baking sheet and place the pizza dough on it. Using fingers and the palms of your hands to stretch out the dough into a 13 x 9-inch rectangle (it need not be even). Stretch out the second ball of dough on another oiled baking sheet. Working with one stretched-out piece at a time, using both hands, gently lift the dough rectangle from the baking sheet. Drape it onto the grill over the hottest part of the fire. Within a minute or so, the under side of the dough will crisp, darken and harden, and the top will puff slightly. Turn the dough over with tongs or two spatulas and move it to the cooler side of the grill.

Quickly brush the top of the pizza with 1 tablespoon of olive oil. Sprinkle half the pizza cheese on the crust. Cover with pizza sauce and add toppings. Slide the pizza back over the hotter part of the grill, rotating to ensure even cooking. Cook until the underside is slightly charred and the cheese is melted, 2 to 4 minutes.

Remove the pizza from the grill, cut into serving pieces, and serve with Aspen Valley Winery's Merlot while you repeat the procedure with the second stretched-out piece of dough.

Makes two pizzas.

Serves 2 to 4

Alta's Notes: This "crunchy" crust pizza would be less time consuming if you have a bread machine that would automatically take care of the first three steps. Our grill seemed too hot, and really blackened the crust; we had more success using the top shelf. In the summer when you have a "hankering" for pizza, this would keep the heat out of the kitchen.

Recipe provided by Patrick Leto

AUGUSTINA'S WINERY'S CAMPSITE CORNISH GAME HENS

Ingredients

2 Cornish Game hens, frozen
1½ cups pre-cooked brown rice
1 Granny Smith apple, cored and diced
½ cup raisins or other dried fruit
½ cup cashew nuts, optional

Method

This from Marianne: "Hike to campsite. Spend remainder of the day hiking, playing, fishing, or reading. By then, the game hens should be thawed out. Get a decent little campfire going. Drink some Irish whiskey. Prepare game hens by stuffing cavity with a mixture of rice, diced apple, dried fruit, and nuts. Wrap in aluminum foil and bury in a bed of coals. Drink red wine and swap stories with your backpacking companion. If you've got a decent bed of coals, the hens should be done in 45 minutes."

Enjoy with a bottle of Ruby (her backpacking wine).

Serves 2

Reminder: "Be sure to pack out all of your trash."

Alta's Notes: I didn't have time to backpack, so I tested this on the grill. I added 2 tablespoons of orange juice to the rice stuffing mixture and lightly coated the outside of the bird with olive oil! I wrapped it in heavy-duty foil, and in 45 minutes I had a moist bird. Easy! I also had leftover rice mixture to which I added a little olive oil, chilled it, and the next day I added a small can of drained tuna to it. *Voilá,* lunch. Two easy meals.

Recipe provided by Marianne Walter

BAHARAV VINEYARDS' MEDITERRANEAN ROSEMARY LEG OF LAMB

Ingredients

5- to 6-pound bone-in leg of lamb
½ cup extra virgin olive oil
4 to 6 cloves of garlic, pressed
Salt and freshly ground pepper
1 sprig of fresh rosemary as long as the width of the roast
1 sprig of fresh thyme
2 cups Baharav's Chardonnay

Method

Ask your butcher to de-bone the leg of lamb.

In a little bowl mix the olive oil, pressed garlic, salt and pepper. Put the rosemary sprig in the center of the de-boned leg and pour about half of the oil mixture over it. Roll up the leg and tie it with a cord. Put the tied up leg in an ovenproof oval dish (I prefer stoneware), brush it with the remaining oil mixture and top with a sprig of thyme.

Bake in a preheated oven on high (400°F) for about 20 minutes. Add one glass of chardonnay to the bottom of the dish and reduce oven temperature to 350°F. Bake for about an hour and fifteen minutes, depending on desired level of doneness (check with meat thermometer), gradually adding the second glass of wine while basting the leg in the accumulating juices. When ready, slice and serve.

Serves 6 to 8 adults

"This is our favorite red and white wine dish; you cook the lamb in white wine, and eat it with the red. Our favorite side dishes are asparagus, carrot strips, and fennel-bulb strips boiled in water, and dabbed with butter, salt and fresh basil, accompanied by an herbed wild rice pilaf. We recommend a Cabernet Franc-Merlot or just Merlot with this excellent dish."—*Eva Baharav*

Alta's Notes: I used a 3½-pound roast and needed a little less cooking time. It served 4 adults with some left over. The meat was flavorful and tender and because I love herbs, I would probably use two sprigs of rosemary. Yum!

Recipe provided by Eva Baharav

J. A. BALISTRERI VINEYARDS' CRAB CIOPPINO

Ingredients

4 Dungeness crabs, cleaned and cracked
¼ cup olive oil
1 cup onion, chopped
1 teaspoon garlic, minced
2 cups water
1 teaspoon salt
2 tablespoons fresh lemon juice
½ cup parsley, chopped
1 cup Balistreri Chardonnay

Method

In a large pan sauté onion in olive oil. When onion is tender, add garlic and fry until golden. Add water and remaining ingredients, except the crab, and bring to a boil. Add crab, cover and shake pan to coat crab with mixture. Steam just until crab is hot throughout.

Serve with fresh Italian bread.

Alta's Notes: Ask your butcher how to crack the crab or maybe you'll luck out like I did and he/she will do it for you. I only used two crabs, but all the broth. The temptation was to dip bread and soak up all of that delectable liquid. This is really a quick and easy dish to impress your family or friends. I also served a green salad and Chardonnay to accompany it. *Buon appetito!*

Recipe provided by John Balistreri

J. A. BALISTRERI VINEYARDS' FLAMED STEAK

Ingredients

2 pounds sirloin steak
½ cup butter
2 tablespoons garlic, minced
2 tablespoons black pepper, freshly ground
½ teaspoon salt
2 teaspoons Worcestershire sauce
1 cup fresh parsley, chopped
1 cup Balistreri's Syrah
½ cup brandy

Method

Cut sirloin in 2- to 3-inch pieces. Slice pieces so they are approximately ¼ inch thick. Pound each piece very thin to 1/8 inch (a baseball size smooth rock with a flat side works well). Have all other ingredients prepared and premeasured before starting to cook. Have a match ready.

In a large heavy skillet over medium high heat, melt half of the butter to sizzling. Add half of the garlic. Place half of the meat pieces on top of sizzling garlic. Sprinkle with half of the ground pepper and salt. Quickly turn meat with a fork. Splash meat with half of the Worcestershire and half of the parsley. Remove meat and with a spatula scrape most of the garlic, etc. from pan to platter. Repeat in same skillet with remaining meat.

Return all meat back to skillet, add all of the wine and heat to boiling. Add brandy and immediately light surface with a match. After flames subside, serve quickly with fresh Italian bread and Balistreri's Syrah, which complements this dish with its spicy black peppery taste.

Alta's Notes: This dish has showmanship. Being timid about flames in my all-white kitchen, I took the pan outside and used the barbecue's side burner. It worked and the flambé was pretty to watch. By the way, that 2 tablespoons of black pepper took quite a while to grind. Make sure to have everything ready because the actual cooking time is very short. Some colorful vegetables round out this dish.

Recipe provided by John Balistreri

BOOKCLIFF VINEYARDS' VEAL STEW IN PUFF PASTRY

Ingredients

1½ pounds veal stew meat, trimmed if necessary and cubed
6 to 7 cups water
¼ pound (approximately) butter for sautéing
½ onion, peeled and chopped
1 pint box of mushrooms, cleaned and chopped
3 tablespoons flour
1 teaspoon dry basil
Salt and pepper to taste
1 tablespoon fresh lemon juice
1 teaspoon Worcestershire sauce
¼ cup or more white wine
1 package Pepperidge Farm frozen puff pastry shells
1 lemon, sliced, for garnish

Method

Cook veal in water with a pinch of salt until soft, about 30 minutes. Sauté onion in butter; add mushrooms and continue sautéing. Add flour, basil and half the liquid from the meat. Add salt, pepper, lemon juice, Worcestershire sauce and white wine to taste. Add meat. Sauce needs to cover meat well. Cook on medium-low heat for 30 minutes. Add more liquid and adjust spices if necessary.

Bake shells according to directions on the box. Take the lids off the shells.

To serve, fill shells generously and allow stew to overflow on the plate. Put lids back on and add a slice of lemon on the side. Put Worcestershire sauce on the table for individual additions. Serve with Bookcliff Vineyards Chardonnay.

Serves 4 adults

Alta's Notes: I used fresh basil (six leaves), torn in small pieces, at the beginning of the cooking time and six more, stirred in just a few minutes before serving. Ulla says you could use lemon juice or wine in the sauce, but I chose to use both. I added about 3½ cups meat liquid, and it took 45 minutes to cook down to fairly thick gravy. It does look elegant and tastes that way too. Top off the dish with a squeeze of lemon or Worcestershire.

Recipe provided by Ulla Merz

CARLSON VINEYARDS' TYRANNOSAURUS RED SPAGHETTI SAUCE

Ingredients

¼ cup olive oil
¼ cup butter
4 medium size onions, chopped
4 cloves of garlic, finely chopped
1 cups celery tops, chopped
1 green pepper, finely chopped
¼ pound mushrooms, chopped
1 teaspoon dry basil
1 teaspoon dry rosemary
½ teaspoon ground pepper
2 teaspoons salt
1 pound Italian sausage, sliced
1 pound lean ground beef
1 pound fresh ground pork
1 20-ounce can diced tomatoes
Two 6-ounce cans tomato paste
2 cups Carson Vineyards Tyrannosaurus Red Wine

Method

Sauté onions in olive oil and butter until golden. Add garlic and sauté 2 minutes more. Add celery tops, green pepper, mushrooms and seasonings; sauté well, stirring often. Set aside.

Brown meats in a large, heavy pan. Add sautéed veggies and mix well. Add tomatoes, tomato paste and wine. Stir until well mixed. Bring to boil; lower heat and simmer for 3 hours. Serve over spaghetti.

Serves 10 to 12 people

"A hearty, rich, aromatic flavor-blend, perfected by Carlson Vineyards' Tyrannosaurus Red Wine and the patient slow cooking."

—*Mary Carlson*

Alta's Notes: I used fresh rosemary and basil and changed the amounts to 3 tablespoons each. It's your choice to use mild, sweet or hot sausage. I browned each meat separately and drained the fat from them before putting them in a large pot. Prep time is from 45 minutes to 1 hour, but it's worth it. The result is a thick, meaty sauce. It freezes well too; I had three more meals in my freezer.

Recipe provided by Mary Carlson

COLORADO CELLARS' CHARDONNAY COOKING WINE SUGGESTIONS

Ingredients

Colorado Cellars makes a line of cooking-related products. Below is a list of uses for its Colorado Chardonnay printed on the label.

Method

From the wine label: "Colorado Cellars' Lemon/Pepper Chardonnay is the most versatile blend in our line. Brush it on chicken, fish, pork chops or ribs before grilling (even add to your BBQ sauce). Excellent for salmon. Mix with mayo for a flavorful artichoke dip. Thicken with cream and Parmesan cheese, pour over linguini and top with broccoli, cauliflower, pea pods, artichokes and tomatoes."

Alta's Notes: Keep this softly flavored Chardonnay on the shelf for whenever you need a little white cooking wine for a recipe.

Recipe provided by Padte Turley

CORLEY VINEYARDS' SAUTÉED CHICKEN TIDBITS WITH ARTICHOKES AND MUSHROOMS

Ingredients

2 pounds chicken breast, skinned, boned and cut into bite-size pieces
½ cup flour
⅓ cup olive oil
2 teaspoons garlic, finely minced
1 to 1½ teaspoons salt
¾ teaspoon white pepper (use black pepper if you don't have white)
Two 14-ounce cans of artichokes, (unmarinated in water); drain well and cut into bite size pieces
2 cups (16 ounces) mushrooms, quartered or cut into thick slices
1 cup Lorinda's Chardonnay (Corley Vineyards, of course), or other dry white wine

Method

Preheat a large saucepan over medium high heat. Add oil. In a large bowl, toss chicken in flour until well coated. Shake off excess flour and add chicken to oil. Add garlic. Season with half of the salt and half of the pepper. Mix well. Brown on all sides. Add artichoke hearts and mushrooms. Mix together well, lower heat and simmer 10 to 15 minutes. Taste and adjust salt and pepper, adding the remainder of the pepper and a little more salt.

Says Lorinda: "I typically pre-measure the salt and pepper and a little at a time after the initial measure. You can always add more, but can't take it out!"

Add Lorinda's Chardonnay, stir well and simmer 15 to 20 minutes, stirring periodically to prevent any sticking to the pan. Taste once more and adjust seasoning. As an entrée, serve with garlic mashed potatoes and steamed broccoli and carrots. As an appetizer—just serve and enjoy!

Serves 5 easily with side dishes; more on its own.

Alta's Notes: You'll need a large, heavy frying pan to make this. When the artichokes and mushrooms are added, there's a considerable mound in the pan. Not to worry, it cooks down. This a delightful blend of flavors. I prefer not to simmer it quite so long to keep the pieces more distinct. Lorinda didn't say, but I would serve it with the Chardonnay also.

Recipe provided by Lorinda Corley

COTTONWOOD CELLARS' SWISS CHEESE FONDUE

Ingredients

2 cups white wine (Olathe Winery Gewürztraminer), divided
Lemon juice, a few drops
½ pound each Emmenthaler and Gruyère cheeses, grated
3 tablespoons flour
3 tablespoons Kirsch (clear cherry brandy)
1 tablespoon butter
1 clove garlic, peeled
Freshly ground black pepper, nutmeg, and salt to taste
1 large loaf of sourdough or French bread with a hard crust

Method

Rub garlic on interior of fondue pot or chafing dish (mince remainder and add to fondue). Pour in 1 cup of the wine, add lemon juice, and bring to a simmer over moderate heat. Combine cheeses and flour and gradually add them to the wine mixture, using a fork or a wooden spoon. When cheese is melted, add remaining wine, Kirsch, butter and spices. Transfer to warmer or over hot water. Do not boil—keep at a low simmer.

Cut bread into 1-inch cubes and dip into mixture with skewers or fondue forks.

Serve with Olathe Winery Gewürztraminer or Johannesburg Riesling. At the end of the evening, scrape off the crusted cheese at the bottom and eat it on bread.

Serves 4 to 6 as a main course or more at a party

"I have tried this with a dry white wine, but it seemed too harsh to me. The off-dry 'Gewürz' adds lovely spices and mellows the cheese." —*Diana Reed*

Alta's Notes: I prefer to start with 1 teaspoon of Kirsch, adding more to taste. Unlike some other recipes, this method of adding all the cheese to half the wine works well. You might consider also having bite-size vegetables to dip, such as cherry or grape tomatoes, chunks of apple, lightly steamed cauliflower or broccoli florets. Wonderfully easy.

Recipe provided by Diana Reed

McELMO CANYON RELLENOS

Ingredients

2 to 3 McElmo Canyon Poblano chiles per person, roasted and peeled
Colby Jack marbled cheese, grated
1 onion, diced
1 egg for every 2 chiles, whites and yolks separated
Vegetable oil
Flour in a flat dish

Method

Clean seeds from inside chiles. Take some grated cheese and diced onion and press them together into an oval shape and fill each chile. Whip egg whites until stiff peaks form. Whip yolks until fluffed. Fold the whites and yolks together gently. DO NOT WHIP.

Put vegetable oil in a large frying pan and heat oil to 350°F. Roll the stuffed chiles in flour and then dip in egg mixture to coat completely. Gently put them in the hot oil and cook them until they are golden brown and then flip to the other side. Remove and place on plate.

Cover rellenos with your favorite green chile sauce (Stokes canned green chile is okay). Serve with beans of choice and Crooked Creek White Table Wine.

Alta's Notes: To roast chiles, cut off tips (to keep them from exploding) and put on hot grill or under broiler until skins are blistered or blackened on all sides. Put them in a plastic bag to steam and get cool enough to handle. Remove the chiles from the bag and peel skin from stem downward. My chiles were almost too tender and fell apart a little. Don't worry. This amazing light batter clings and keeps all together.

This is one of Brad's favorites and he loads on the sauce. I like just a little not to cover up the light crunch with the chile-cheese flavor. After having lived in Mexico and New Mexico, we must have guacamole with this kind of meal.

Recipe provided by Guy Drew Vineyards

PLUM CREEK CELLARS' BEEF BOURGUIGNON

Ingredients

3 pounds steak, cut into 1½ inch pieces
½ cup flour
1 teaspoon salt
½ teaspoon pepper
¼ cup butter
¼ cup olive oil
¼ cup cognac
5 carrots, coarsely chopped
2 medium yellow onions, coarsely chopped
1 leek, coarsely chopped
5 sprigs parsley, chopped
4 cloves of garlic, finely minced
⅓ pound bacon, diced
1 teaspoon thyme
3 tablespoons tomato paste
1 cup Plum Creek Cellars' Cabernet Franc or Merlot
2 cups beef broth
Salt and pepper, freshly ground, to taste
20 small white pearl onions
¼ pound butter
1 to 1½ pounds fresh mushrooms, sliced

Method

Dredge meat in flour, salt and pepper. In a large heavy pan, brown meat on all sides in butter and oil over high heat. Do this in small batches, adding butter and oil if necesssary. As meat is browned, place it in a 5-quart casserole or deep roasting pan. Deglaze pan by pouring cognac into it and stirring to loosen particles. Pour gravy over the meat.

To the same pan add carrots, chopped onions, leek, parsley, garlic and bacon. Cook stirring until vegetables and bacon are lightly browned. Skim off bacon fat. Add thyme and tomato paste to pan, stir and add all to the beef. Add Plum Creek wine and beef broth to barely cover meat and mix well. Taste for salt and pepper and add if necessary.

Cover casserole and bake for 1 hour in an oven preheated to 325°F. Stir occasionally and add more beef broth if needed. Meanwhile, peel pearl onions by dropping in boiling water for 1 minute

(recipe cont. on next page)

and slipping off skins. Brown them in ¼ cup butter. Remove from pan and then sauté mushrooms. Add onions and mushrooms to beef casserole and bake 1 more hour.

Serves 6 to 8 adults

Alta's Notes: I used sirloin and low salt bacon. Different bacons will change the taste. Personal preference—I would have liked more carrots. Possibly because of a pan size difference, I needed more broth and wine to cover the beef and vegetables. I served this with crusty bread, a green salad and Merlot. This is a filling "company" dinner. Enjoy!

Recipe provided by Doug and Sue Phillips

PUESTA DEL SOL WINERY'S GRILLED MARINATED LAMB CHOPS

Ingredients

2 to 3 pounds lamb chops, 1 to 1½ inches thick
2 cups Puesta del Sol Pinot Noir or other red wine
2 bay leaves
½ cup fresh mint, chopped (or 2 tablespoon mint jelly)
½ teaspoon black peppercorns
¼ teaspoon whole allspice
¼ teaspoon whole cloves
2 garlic cloves, pressed and chopped
1 yellow onion, thinly sliced

Method

Combine all ingredients in a large container with a lid. Add lamb chops. Cover tightly and refrigerate overnight or at least 3 hours, turning the chops frequently. Remove the meat from the marinade and discard the marinade. Grill the chops and serve with the dill and cucumber sauce on the side (see recipe on the following page). This main dish can be served with pita bread, a Greek salad and Puesta del Sol Pinot Noir to make a lovely dinner with a Greek flavor.

DILL AND CUCUMBER SAUCE

Ingredients

2 cups cucumbers, grated
1¼ cups plain yogurt
2 tablespoons fresh or dried dill weed
4 garlic cloves, pressed and chopped
1 teaspoon lemon juice

Method

Combine all ingredients in a medium bowl. Cover and refrigerate for at least 1 hour. The sauce can be made up to a day ahead of time.

Alta's Notes: This made a delightful meal. I used 1 inch or thicker lamb chops and marinated them for 3½ hours. They needed to cook on medium coals for 18 minutes total to be medium-rare. There were hints of mint and spices, and the meat was juicy and tender.

I peeled and seeded the cucumber before grating, knowing they were juicy; for this reason, I also made yogurt cheese (put a coffee filter in a strainer over a bowl, put yogurt in the filter, refrigerate for a couple of hours, and discard the liquid). The result is a firmer yogurt. The amount of garlic can be adjusted to taste. The sauce is cool and refreshing.

Recipes provided by Pam Petersen

ROCKY HILL WINERY'S BARBECUED FLANK STEAK

Ingredients

½ to 2 pounds flank steak

Marinade:

½ cup vegetable oil
¼ cup Red Mountain Merlot
2 tablespoons brown sugar
2 tablespoons Worcestershire sauce
1 tablespoon lemon juice
3 cloves garlic, minced

Method

Place steak in a shallow glass dish. Combine the marinade ingredients and pour over steak. Cover and put in fridge. Marinate overnight, turning once.

Remove steak from marinade and put it in the center of a preheated barbecue grill. Cook for 5 minutes on each side; steak will be browned on both sides and pink in the center. (Prolonged cooking will toughen the steak.)

Prepare your favorite vegetables, toss with melted butter, herbs, salt, and pepper. Wrap in foil "parcels." Cook in the oven or on the barbecue.

Serves 4 to 6

Alta's Notes: As a personal preference, I used less than a half-cup of canola oil. You could also cut down on the brown sugar if you don't like it too sweet.

I used individual-size double-foil packets and sprayed the center of it with olive oil. Then put in peeled and sliced onion, topped with ¼-inch slices of red potatoes. The portions should match each individual's appetite. Spray lightly with olive oil, sprinkle with fresh rosemary leaves, salt and pepper. These packets needed 20 to 25 minutes to cook. This is a quick and easy supper; consider marinating Sunday night and coming home to an almost-finished meal.

Recipe provided by Dave Fansler

STEAMBOAT SPRINGS CELLARS' GRILLED TURKEY

Ingredients

12- to 14-pound fresh turkey

Brine:

3 quarts water
2 cups brown sugar
1 cup maple syrup
¾ cup coarse salt
3 whole heads garlic, cloves separated (but not peeled), bruised
6 large bay leaves
1½ cups fresh unpeeled ginger, coarsely chopped
2 teaspoons dried chile flakes
1½ cups soy sauce
Fresh thyme sprigs to taste

Olive oil for brushing

Method

Combine all brine ingredients in a 5-gallon pot. Bring to simmer, remove from heat, let cool completely. Remove neck and giblets and rinse turkey. Put turkey in cold brine; add water if necessary. Refrigerate 2 to 4 days, turning bird twice daily.

To Cook Turkey:

Remove the turkey from the brine and pat dry. Lightly brush it with olive oil. Light the grill and give it sufficient time to heat up. Put 1-inch-deep drip pan under bird. If using coals, put coals on either side of pan. Put ½ cup of wood chips in a double layer of aluminum foil over coals.

Place turkey on highest rack, breast side up. Regulate vents to keep a little smoke coming out and coals burning slowly. Check every half-hour or so. Keep temperature between 275°F and 325°F. Cook 3 to 3½ hours. Internal temperature should reach 155°F. Test with an instant-read thermometer or cut a small incision between the leg and thigh, just to see if juices run clear.

Remove from grill for 20 minutes before carving. Serve with Chardonnay or Fish Creek Falls (wine name) from Steamboat Springs Cellars. Tom says: "This takes a while to make, but it is well worth the effort. The meat falls off the bones."

Alta's Notes: Cooking an entire turkey on a grill is not something that I would normally attempt. However, I did it! I had some setbacks ordering a fresh turkey from my local store. After some frustrations, I decided to use two fresh turkey breasts. Because there's so much marinade, it took 30 minutes or more to reach the simmering stage, but it took longer to cool (which I expedited by putting the pan in a sink filled with ice water). I wrote reminder notes to myself to remember to go down to our extra refrigerator and turn the bird.

I have a gas grill, and the birds were so juicy I had to keep changing the aluminum foil I formed into a drip pan. At 1 hour and 45 minutes my grill ran out of gas, but the breasts were almost done. Like all turkey baking, time depends on the size of the bird and your grill or oven. I wrapped them in foil and finished them in a 325°F oven for about 30 minutes. The result? Moist, subtly flavored turkey and packets of cooked turkey in the freezer. And didn't I feel accomplished?

Recipe provided by Tom Williams

STONEY MESA WINERY'S BROIL-ROASTED CORNISH GAME HENS IN WINE

Ingredients

3 Rock Cornish Hens
Salt and pepper
Butter, melted
1 cup Swiss cheese, coarsely grated
1 head of garlic, separated into cloves and peeled
½ cup Stoney Mesa Sauvignon Blanc
1 pound fresh mushrooms, trimmed, cleaned and quartered

Method

Cut hens up backbone; spread flat and with skin side up pound breast flat. Salt and pepper each hen and brush with melted butter. Preheat broiler. Put hens skin side down on broiler pan about 3 inches from heat source and brown for about 5 minutes. Turn over and brown on skin side.

Preheat oven to 400°F. Place birds skin side up in roasting pan. Divide cheese among chickens sprinkling it on top and scatter the garlic around the pan. Pour in enough wine to reach ¼-inch level. Place pan in upper middle oven and cook 20 minutes, basting periodically. Add mushrooms and continue to cook until birds are tender and juices run clear.

Serves 6

Alta's Notes: You may need up to a half bottle of wine to reach the ¼-inch level, depending on the size of your pan. Drink the rest with dinner, of course. The skin is brown and very tasty; the mushrooms and garlic take on wonderful flavors.

Recipe provided by Donna Neal

TERROR CREEK WINERY'S COUNTRY CHICKEN CASSEROLE

Ingredients

1 medium-size cooked chicken, skin and bones removed
1 pound button mushrooms, sautéed in butter
1 cup each cooked peas, carrots, and potatoes

Sauce:

½ cup butter
½ cup flour
2 cups chicken stock
1 cup Terror Creek Dry Riesling, or other dry white wine
½ cup dry sherry
1 cup cream
½ cup chopped parsley

Method

Preheat oven to 350°F. Melt butter, stir in flour; keep stirring while adding all wet ingredients and parsley. Season to taste. Continue to cook over medium heat until sauce thickens.

Assemble by placing all veggies and "nice size" chicken morsels into casserole, alternating layers. Finish with a layer of chicken on top. Pour the sauce over all (sauce should cover other ingredients). Bake uncovered at 350°F for about 45 minutes.

Serves 4 to 5 hungry people.

Alta's Notes: I peeled and cubed the red potatoes in 1-inch chunks. I cooked my vegetables in the microwave until they were crisp-tender. The sauce needs to be a medium-to-thick white sauce. There is a generous amount of sauce and we might have liked more peas and carrots. This is more of a Sunday special than a week night casserole.

Recipe provided by Joan Mathewson

ITALIAN SAUSAGE WITH GREENS À LA TRAIL RIDGE WINERY

Ingredients

Extra virgin olive oil as required
½ white or yellow onion, chopped finely
1 to many cloves of garlic, to taste—chop them fairly coarsely, so they do not burn
1 pound sweet or hot Italian sausage, casing removed (If you're in the area, we strongly recommend the sausage made by Dominic and Teresa Sansotta of Belfiore Italian Sausage, 3161 West 38th Avenue in Denver.)
1 bunch mustard greens, stalks finely chopped and leaves a bit more coarsely chopped
½ teaspoon fennel seeds, or more to taste
⅓ cup Trail Ridge Lemberger (okay, if you want to drink all the Lemberger, use any good red wine)
Balsamic vinegar to taste

Method

Heat about ¼ cup olive oil over medium heat in a large skillet. Add the onions and garlic and sauté for a few minutes until they soften. Add the sausage, breaking into chunks with the back of a spoon. Sauté the sausage, stirring frequently, for a few more minutes, until it is lightly browned. Then add the mustard greens and fennel seeds. At first, the skillet will be very full, but the greens will cook down a great deal. Continue to cook and stir the skillet for about five more minutes. Then deglaze the pan with the ⅓ cup of wine and continue to cook until the wine has largely evaporated. Reduce the heat to very low, cover the pan and let the dish simmer for about 10 minutes, while you either prepare the frittata or cook the penne. Then drizzle balsamic vinegar to taste (we like about ¼ cup or so) over the sausage and greens. Stir and serve with extra grated Parmigiana Reggiano on the side.

Serves 4

"As you enjoy the food, notice how the fennel picks up an anise aroma in the Lemberger, and the slight bitterness of the greens sets off the berryish acidity of the wine. We think this is a wonderful, simple dish that you can enjoy again and again. At Trail Ridge, we are always interested in trying new recipes to pair our wines with interesting foods. During a couple of 'research sessions' (you might call it 'dinner') over the winter months, we developed the recipe. Its roots are in southern Italy, but the flavors seem to call out the best in our Lemberger. Of course, Trail Ridge Lemberger is the ideal wine to accompany it." —*Tim Merrick*

Alta's Notes: This was our first time to have mustard greens and we loved them in this dish. I used 6 large cloves of garlic and wished I'd used more than ½ teaspoon of fennel. I served it over penne. A new taste treat for us.

Recipe provided by Tim Merrick

TWO RIVERS WINERY'S SHRIMP PICAYUNE

Ingredients

6 large raw shrimp per person

Sauce:

1 cup olive oil
¾ cup clarified butter
½ cup liquid brown sugar
2 tablespoons Worcestershire sauce
3 bay leaves
½ cup fresh lemon juice
½ cup plus 2 tablespoons vermouth
1 tablespoon plus 1 teaspoon orégano leaves
1 tablespoon plus 1 teaspoon thyme leaves
1 tablespoon plus 1 teaspoon granulated garlic
1 tablespoon plus 1 teaspoon salt
1 tablespoon plus 1 teaspoon pepper
2 teaspoons cayenne pepper
1 teaspoon ground rosemary
1½ teaspoons Tabasco sauce
¾ teaspoon poultry seasoning

Method

Combine all sauce ingredients and stir well.

To prepare shrimp, peel them and place in a metal or broiler-safe pan. Pour sauce over shrimp (3 ounces per 6 shrimp). Place shrimp under direct broiler heat in your oven for 5 to 7 minutes. Serve with Two Rivers Merlot.

Alta's Notes: To liquefy brown sugar, simply stir in a little hot water. Billie said this was an entrée, but I used half the sauce and a pound of large shrimp as an appetizer for eight people. It was very tasty. The only regret some of us had was that we needed crusty bread to soak up some of that sauce. If I were serving this dish as an entrée, I would use jumbo shrimp or have a smaller appetite.

Recipe provided by Billie Witham

DESSERTS

ALTA'S PEACHES PALISADE

Ingredients

4 fresh peaches (hopefully from Palisade), washed, halved, with a little of the flesh scooped out to make a larger cavity

Filling:

½ cup slivered almonds, toasted
3 tablespoons brown sugar
2½ coconut macaroons, crumbled
1 tablespoon Amaretto or ½ teaspoon almond flavoring
1 egg yolk

Additional ingredients:

Butter
½ cup white wine from your favorite Colorado winery
⅓ cup sliced almonds, toasted

Method

Put all the filling ingredients in a food processor and blend to make a thick, pasty ball. Put peaches cut side up in a buttered glass or ceramic oven-safe dish/pan. Divide filling equally among the peaches, making a little mound. Pour wine around peach halves. Bake at 325°F for 30 minutes. Allow to cool for 5 minutes or more. Put in a bowl and sprinkle with toasted, sliced almonds if desired.

Serves 8 or fewer, depending on individual appetites

Alta's Notes: Although I'm not a winemaker, I had to add something else representing our state's Western Slope fruit. This is a light "summery" dessert.

Recipe provided by Alta Smith

CREEKSIDE CELLARS' RASPBERRY PORT SAUCE

Ingredients

1 (1-pound bag) frozen red or black raspberries or blackberries
2 cups Creekside Cellars Black Muscat Port
1 tablespoon brown sugar or to taste

Method

Put fruit in saucepan; mash it. Add brown sugar and port. Stir often while simmering for an hour or more until the sauce is reduced by half. Serve over cheesecake or ice cream.

Bill Donahue says: "Most of our customers think it's so good that we should bottle it."

Alta's Notes: I reduced it longer and got a sauce that was quite thick. What a simple and delectable addition! My guests and Brad immediately started a list of many desserts on which it would be great, such as flourless chocolate cake. Me? Just give me a spoon.

Recipe provided by Bill and Tim Donahue

REDSTONE MEADERY'S HAPPY COBBLER

Ingredients

1 pint blueberries
1 pint raspberries
1 quart strawberries
Redstone Meadery's Black Raspberry Nectar
¼ cup plus 1 tablespoon sugar, divided
1 tablespoon fresh lemon juice
Finely grated zest of half a lemon
2 cups unbleached all purpose flour
A pinch of salt
1 tablespoon baking powder
⅓ cup plus 3 tablespoons of softened butter
1 egg
⅓ cup milk

Method

Soak berries in nectar for 5 to 6 hours. Preheat oven to 425°F. Drain berries and combine with sugar, lemon juice and lemon zest. Toss lightly in a bowl to combine. After combined, place fruit mixture in a medium-size glass casserole dish.

In a separate bowl, mix together flour, salt, baking powder and 1 tablespoon of sugar. After mixing, work ⅓ cup butter in with fingers or a pastry blender until it resembles coarse crumbs. Separately beat egg and milk mixture together; then add to flour mixture, creating a dough. Roll out dough into shape of baking dish. Place dough over berries and tuck in around the sides. With additional 3 tablespoons of softened butter, spread a light coat over crust to help make the crust golden. Lightly sprinkle sugar on crust. Bake for 35 to 45 minutes. Let cool.

If you would like a bottom dough as well, double the dough recipe and place dough on bottom of the dish. Bake separately for 5 to 7 minutes, then add berries and continue with the recipe.

Serves 8

Alta's Notes: The fruit picks up a lot of the "wine" flavor; you could soak the fruit a shorter time. I added 2 tablespoons of instant tapioca to the sugared fruit, so it would be a little thicker. This is a thick biscuit dough. If you prefer, you could cut the recipe for the topping in half and roll it or drop by spoonfuls on top of the fruit.

Recipe provided by David Myers

ROCKY MOUNTAIN MEADERY'S ROYAL "PEACHES AND HONEY MOUSSE"

Ingredients

1 envelope unflavored gelatin
½ cup milk
½ cup Peaches 'n Honey wine
2 cups light vanilla nonfat yogurt
6 peach halves
Nutmeg (optional)
Raspberries, thawed for garnish

Method

Sprinkle gelatin over cold milk in a blender and soften for 5 minutes. Bring wine to a boil and pour over gelatin mixture and blend. Add yogurt and continue to blend. Pour into each of six dessert bowls over a peach half. Sprinkle with nutmeg. Refrigerate a couple of hours. Serve with a topping of raspberries.

Serves 6

Alta's Notes: This can be made totally fat free since it doesn't have the eggs and sugar of an actual mousse. This is easy and very mild, so you may want a little almond extract; therefore, the nutmeg gives it a punch and the raspberries give it color and another flavor.

Recipe provided by Rocky Mountain Meadery from their contest winner, Barbara Scott

ST. KATHRYN CELLARS' BLUEBERRY BLISS SORBET

Ingredients

1 cup blueberry jam
½ cup fresh lemon juice
½ teaspoon lemon zest
1¼ cup water
¾ cup St. Kathryn Cellars Blueberry Bliss wine

Method

Combine jam, lemon juice, zest, water and wine in a bowl. Either freeze according to directions for an ice-cream maker or pour into a flat glass or metal dish and freeze until solid, 6 hours or overnight. Cut into chunks, process in a food processor or blender just until smooth. Refreeze for at least 2 hours before serving.

Makes about 1 quart

Alta's Notes: I used the long method instead of my Donvier and found that you need to put it in a very cold part of the freezer and serve it quickly. I used a "spreadable" fruit jam and I'm sure it would be improved with a sweet blueberry jam. Consider serving in small wine glasses as a palate-cleansing course, especially after something spicy. Garnish with a sprig of mint, a few blueberries or an edible flower.

Recipe provided by Connie and Fred Strothman

GLOSSARY OF WINE TERMS

Acidity—The tartness in a wine due to natural fruit acids. Acidity protects wine from spoilage but also determines its overall taste balance.

Aftertaste—The impression the wine leaves after it is swallowed. Sometimes called the "finish" of a wine.

Aroma—Fragrance of the wine, which comes from the grapes used to make it.

Astringent—The sensation of dryness in the mouth, making you pucker your lips. Caused by high tannins in the wine.

Austere—A wine characteristic referring to a hard or restrained fruit character.

Balance—Relationship of alcohol, acid, tannin and flavor of a wine, varying according to its style and origin, but usually connoting a flavor where none of the characters stand out.

Big—Description of full-bodied wines with rich flavors. Powerful.

Bitter—Normally regarded as a fault in wines.

Body—Fullness of a wine in the mouth. The overall weight and texture of the wine, sometimes related to alcoholic content.

Bouquet—Smells caused by the barrel or bottle aging, as opposed to "aroma."

Brix—The term used in measuring sugar content in grapes, grape juice or wine. Most grapes are harvested at around 20 to 25 Brix, which provides an alcohol level of 11.5 to 14 percent.

Brut—Dry to nearly dry Champagne or sparkling wine. Has 1.5 percent or less residual sugar.

Buttery—The rich flavor or smoothness of a wine, similar to the oiliness of butter. Usually used to refer to aged white wines.

Chewy—A "winespeak" word referring to the heavy or thick feel of the wine in the mouth, often caused by tannins.

Complex—A wine with many aromas and flavors. Normally, complex wines are highly sought after.

Corked, corky—A bad wine that smells of cork.

Crisp—Refers to lively taste of a white wine.

Delicate—Subtle fragrance, flavor and body.
Dry—Normally a wine with less than 0.5 percent residual sugar. The opposite of sweet.
Dull—Without character, often lacking proper acidity.
Earthy—A smell or taste that reminds one of earth. A little can be good; too much is bad.
Elegant—Not heavy; a refined taste.
Fat—Full-bodied. Sometimes called "fleshy."
Finish—Sensation of taste and texture during or after swallowing. Often synonymous with "aftertaste."
Firm—Balanced structure, so tightly knit that individual elements are not distinguishable.
Flowery—Flower aromas.
Fruity—Indicates lots of fruit flavor, sometimes grapes but also apple, black currant, cherry, citrus, pear, peach, raspberry or strawberry.
Green—A wine made from grapes that haven't ripened, lacking fruit flavor.
Harsh—Excessive tannin or acid, which gives wine too much bite.
Herbaceous—A tasting term referring to flavors that resemble fresh grass, especially in Sauvignon Blanc, and the green pepper of some Cabernet.
Intricate—Subtle flavor and aroma.
Legs—The rivulets that run down the inside of the glass after it is swirled. Caused by the glycerin and alcohol in a wine. Lack of legs means a "thin" wine.
Lively—Usually refers to acidity that gives a positive "zing" to wine.
Mature—Ready to drink, well-aged.
Muscular—Robust, powerful body and flavor; pronounced fruit taste.
Musty—Stale or rank aromas.
Noble—Usually refers to the "noble" grapes associated with the world's (meaning French) best wines: Cabernet Sauvignon, Merlot, Chardonnay, Sauvignon Blanc, Semillon and Riesling. Others include Syrah and the Italian Nebbiolo and Sangiovese.
Nose—Overall smell of a wine, combining aroma and bouquet.
Oaky—The smell and taste, sometimes akin to vanilla, cedar or toasted flavors, which come from aging wine in oak barrels.
Off-dry—A level of sweetness just above dry. A slight sweetness.
Oxidized—Flat, stale; spoiled by overexposure to air.
Robust—A full-bodied wine with an unrefined rough texture.
Round—Smooth and well-developed flavors.

Sharp—Biting tannins or acidic.
Smoky—A flavor associated with some types of oak aging.
Soft—Describes a low level of acid and/or tannin.
Sour—Sharp acid or vinegar taste.
Structure—The totality of the wine's composition and individual elements.
Supple—A wine that is ready to drink. Its flavor is mature.
Tannin—Chemical from skins, seeds and stems of grapes that gives red wine an astringent "puckering" taste. Most prominent in red wines and usually mellows with age.
Vanilla—The flavor sometimes imparted to wine by aging in oak.
Woody—The excess aroma of wood acquired by too much aging in oak.
Yeasty—Often associated with secondary fermentation, providing an aroma of bread.

FESTIVALS, TOURS AND WEBSITES

FESTIVALS

The festivals listed below are places where you can try Colorado wines, sometimes alongside those from other states. The dates are approximate only because they change from year to year. Most charge an admission fee. There have been many attempts to establish a continuing Colorado wine festival on the Front Range, but these have not yet been successful, although we expect efforts to continue. Watch local media for special tastings, which are sometimes held with major liquor stores or hotels.

JUNE

WINEFEST, MARRIOTT HOTEL, FORT COLLINS. Benefiting the Disabled Resource Services Center of Larimer County. About 150 wineries participate, including many from Colorado. Call Supermarket Liquors, 970-221-2428, for information and tickets.

TELLURIDE WINE FESTIVAL, usually features a few Colorado wineries. In 2001 these included Canyon Wind, Cottonwood Cellars and Plum Creek Cellars. Call 800-525-3455 or 970-728-3178; www.telluridewinefestival.org.

FOOD & WINE MAGAZINE CLASSIC AT ASPEN. More of a focus on food than wine, but there is ample opportunity to taste numerous wines. A few Colorado wineries are occasionally represented. You'll get to see the movers and shakers in the food world here. 877-900-WINE; www.foodandwine.com/classic.

SEPTEMBER

COLORADO MOUNTAIN WINEFEST, PALISADE, third weekend. The "showcase" for most Colorado wineries and the first one specifically for the state's wines. Includes winemakers' dinners, music, wine-tasting, tours, food and educational events. The tenth annual Winefest in 2001 included nineteen wineries. 800-704-3667; www.coloradowinefest.com.

OTHER TASTING OPPORTUNITIES

WINES OF COLORADO, which is an off-site tasting room for Minturn Cellars, has the largest collection of the state's wines available for tasting. It is located near Cascade at 8045 West U.S. Highway 24 west of Colorado Springs. It is open 11 A.M.–7 P.M. daily and also offers food. Call 719-684-0900.

TEWKSBURY & CO. in Writer's Square, 1512 Larimer Street, in Denver, has tastings from some wineries, including Plum Creek Cellars. Call 303-825-1880.

HONEYVILLE, 33633 U.S. Highway 550 about 10 miles north of Durango is an off-site tasting room for the Rocky Mountain Meadery. Call 800-676-7690.

TOURS

Three Grand Junction companies offer driving tours of selected wineries in the Grand Valley. Some of the tours include picnics or dinners. Contact Absolute Prestige Limousines at 970-858-8500, Gisdho Shuttle & Limousine Service at 888-226-5031 or Jurassic Tours at 970-256-0884.

WEBSITES

ABOUT COLORADO

Colorado Wine Industry Development Board:
 www.coloradowine.com
Rocky Mountain Association of Vintners and Viticulturalists:
 www.rmavv.org
Grand Junction Convention and Visitors Bureau Guide to
 Wineries: www.visitgrandjunction.com/wine_country.html

GENERAL

The Wine Lovers' Page: www.wine-lovers-page.com
University of California at Davis wine department:
    wineserver.ucdavis.edu
Wines.com: www.wines.com
Wine Spectator magazine: www.winespectator.com
List of wine publications: wines.com/winetrader/996wfp.html
Wine Brats: www.winebrats.org
Directory of wine websites:
    www.vine2wine.com/Introduction.htm
Wine critic Robert Parker's site: www.winetech.com/index.htm

WINE BOOKS

The Colorado Grape Growers Guide, by Richard Hamman, Steve Savage and Harold Larsen. Fort Collins, Colo.: Cooperative Extension Resource Center, Colorado State University, 1998.

From Vines to Wines: The Complete Guide to Growing Grapes and Making Your Own Wine, by Jeff Cox. North Adams, Mass.: Storey Books, 1999.

How and Why to Build a Wine Cellar, by Richard M. Gold, Ph.D. Coquitlan, B.C., Canada: Sandhill Publishers, 1996.

New Sotheby's Wine Encyclopedia: A Comprehensive Reference Guide to the Wines of the World, by Tom Stevenson. New York: DK Publishing, 2001.

The Oxford Companion to Wine, by Jancis Robinson, A. Dinsmoor Webb and Richard Smart. Oxford, England: Oxford University Press, 1999.

The Oxford Companion to the Wines of North America, by Bruce Cass and Jancis Robinson. Foster City, Calif.: IDG Books, 1998.

Windows on the World Complete Wine Course 2002: A Lively Guide, by Kevin Zraly. New York: Sterling Publications, 2001.

Wine for Dummies, by Ed McCarthy and Mary Ewing-Mulligan. Oxford, England: Oxford University Press, 2000.

Wine Science: Principles, Practice, Perception, by Ron S. Jackson. St. Catharine's, Ont. Canada: Brock University Press, 2000.

The World Atlas of Wine, by Hugh Johnson. New York: Simon & Schuster, 1994.

INDEX